ZAC
VERSUS
SADIQ

The fight
to become
London
Mayor

Copyright © Dave Hill, 2016
Published by Double Q Books, 2016.

The right of Dave Hill to be identified as the Author of
the Work has been asserted by him in accordance with
the Copyright, Designs and Patents Act 1988.

All rights reserved.

ISBN 978-1-911079-20-0

This book is sold subject to the condition it shall not,
by way of trade or otherwise, be circulated in any form
or by any means, electronic or otherwise without the
publisher's prior consent.

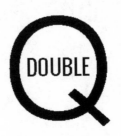

Contents

About the Author

Dave Hill is the Guardian's award-winning London commentator. He lives in East London. He watched the fight through every round.

"There is a reporter in the room. He's a good one: Dave Hill from the Guardian."
– Ken Livingstone
(London Mayor 2000-2008).

"No one could be better placed than Dave Hill to provide an insightful account and analysis of the 2016 battle for London."
– Professor Tony Travers, LSE London.

"Dave Hill is always right."
– Boris Johnson
(London Mayor 2008-2016).

Introduction

London's City Hall is a globular glass building on the south bank of the River Thames, standing across the water from the ancient Tower of London and close to the famous Tower Bridge. Opened in 2002, architect Norman Foster's creation is a symbol of the British capital entering the 21st century as a modern "world city" and the home of its mayor, a new kind of political leader for a metropolis that is booming and growing in such a way and at such a rate that it can look to the rest of the country like a separate nation state.

The position of London Mayor is still very new. It is just 16 years since the office was founded and its powers are limited – too limited in the view of many wise observers - compared with those of counterparts in other countries. Yet they are greater than many people think. The mayor's job is sometimes still dismissed as mere fiddling with bus fares and showing off. Yet the holder of the post presides over a budget bigger than that of many national government departments, has command of a vast transport network through the partner organisation Transport for London, sets the priorities of the Metropolitan Police Service, draws up the master planning framework for the city, can intervene in what gets built there and what gets knocked down, affect a range of environmental issues and have influence over education, health and the arts. Already, the mayoralty is one of the most coveted elected positions in the land.

This book, completed ten days after the election on 5 May, is about the fight to win control of City Hall in 2016. It is about the two men at the centre of that fight. It also about politics, of course, yet also what the contest revealed about the city, about its people and the sort of place it is and could yet be. London's massing dominance sparks resentment and bewilderment. The capital is sometimes seen as a churning vortex of greed, heartlessness and contaminating foreignness. Yet these perceived taints are also claimed as virtues. London's enterprise is seen as admirable, its openness as exciting, its cultural mix as a dazzling mosaic and all of these things as inseparable from its success.

My interest in these things is both professional and personal. For the past eight years, since being asked out of the blue to write regular dispatches about the 2008 mayoral campaign, I've had the honour and the pleasure of being the Guardian's London commentator. It has been easily the best job I've had in the three and a half decades I've been making my living as a journalist. My adult life story too is inextricably entangled with London. As a young man the city offered me escape and possibility. It became where I found true love and where my children were born and have grown. Today, it is not simply my home but a source of infinite fascination: an urban kaleidoscope of deep complexity, unending variety and enthralling change.

London, by its nature, is a weave of millions of different stories, some inspiring, some ugly, some strange. The story of the 2016 mayoral race, which I was deeply immersed in covering for a full year, possessed each of those qualities and illuminated many other stories too. Its two frontrunners, though chasing the same prize, personified very different aspects of city.

I won't patronise readers by pretending that I didn't prefer one of the antagonists named in this book's title to the other from the start. The Guardian is one of that minority of British national – and nowadays international - news outlets that reflects and favours the left of the political spectrum. It is no coincidence that I write for it. My background is different in many ways from the candidate I liked better, not least for beginning in small town England. But I share with him a gratitude to London for enabling me to become someone I would never have become without it. My wife's background too stirred my sympathies with him. She is the London-born daughter of Irish migrants to the city and grew up in a large family during the time of the IRA bombing campaigns. There are certain parallels, as will be seen.

That said, the other frontrunner had his attractions and fascinations too. As well as representing the other side of Britain's principal party political divide, he is from another London entirely, a rarefied, exclusive milieu that few inhabit and even fewer have access too unless they have acquired certain passkeys at birth. But this man had made more single-minded and individual use of the advantages he inherited than most others in such circumstances. His appeal as a candidate lay largely in the prospect of his embedding certain principles and passions in his exercise of the mayoralty's powers and his use of the elevated public platform it provides.

What follows represents my best efforts at capturing the defining events, ideas and themes of the journey of those two men – the Zac and Sadiq of the title – towards election day and the many aspects of London they addressed along the way. If it contains no factual errors, that will be a miracle. I therefore apologise for those in advance.

Finally, some thank yous. Sadly, one is posthumous: to the late Georgina Henry, who commissioned my first London mayoral campaign articles when she was editor of the revolutionary Guardian website then known as Comment is Free. I remain grateful to the Guardian for later making me one of the first of its writers entrusted with a self-published column (initially called Dave Hill's London Blog, now called Dave Hill On London). I'd like to thank I Am Self-Publishing for turning this book around so quickly. Last but definitely not least thanks to my wife, the fabulous Sheila Fitzsimons – she's the true love mentioned above – and my cast of six fantastic children who are, in order of appearance, Laura, Frankie, Nat, Dolores, Conall and Orla.

Dave Hill, 15 May 2016.

<u>One</u>

Contenders

They were in Parliament Square to express opposition to the enlargement of an airport. On this, they stood as one. Otherwise, the contrasts between the two men were stark. Both were close to home in that both had seats in the House of Commons. But photographs of the pair, taken against a backdrop of protest banners and the Palace of Westminster, fixed and dramatized what separated them, even as they shook hands.

Frank Zacharias Robin Goldsmith, known as Zac, towered above Sadiq Aman Khan. Slim and fair, Goldsmith, then aged 40, looked out across the world from a still youthful face that spoke authentically of effortless, inherited English wealth. Women and other judges characterising his type have reached for the word "dreamy". He was noted for his soft voice and unhurried manner. Those who termed him languid did so with a kind of disapproving envy.

The look and posture of 45-year-old Khan hinted at his arrival in the political arena by way of a different path. His South Asian complexion signalled his Pakistani roots, though London was his place of birth. His black hair was fading to grey but the pictures caught a taut, youthful energy as he looked up to meet the other man's courteous, perhaps curious gaze. It said the little guy was not for backing down.

Here they were, the main contestants to become London's next mayor, framed to the point of cliché. How seductive that cliché was.

*****

Goldsmith had entered the world in 1975 in the same, august neighbourhood where he and Khan stood together on that October 2015 day - a Westminster world of power and status and immense financial means. His late father Sir James Goldsmith had been a spectacular figure on the stage of British life, a renegade tycoon. When he died in 1997 he left a fortune to the younger Goldsmith estimated at between £200m and £300m.

Khan's life began in 1970 in the then working-class South London suburb of Earlsfield, near Tooting, after his father Amanullah and mother Sehrun arrived from Pakistan during the second half of the 1960s. He was the fifth of their eight children, all but one of them boys. Amanullah got a job driving a London bus. Sehrun sewed clothes for a living. They lived in a three-bedroom council flat on the post-war, Henry Prince housing estate. The young Khan attended the local Fircroft state primary school and the local comprehensive secondary, Ernest Bevin college, which was named after a famed trade unionist and Labour politician. Like his brothers, he enjoyed sport, especially football, cricket and boxing. After leaving school, he went to the University of North London to study law. His parents later managed to buy a home of their own, but Khan was still sleeping on a bunk bed under their roof at the age of 24 until he married childhood sweetheart Saadiya Ahmed, a fellow solicitor, in 1994. They are still together, and have two daughters.

Goldsmith's educational journey had followed an unconnected course. It began with three different prep schools. The first was King's House in Richmond, the affluent south-west London suburb he had gone on to represent as an MP. Fellow alumni include the former England rugby union captain Lawrence Dallaglio and the comic actor Nigel Planer. The second was the Mall school in nearby Twickenham. Hawtreys in Wiltshire was the third fee-paying educational institution to ready him for public school.

That public school was Eton College, one of England's most famous. His father had attended it too, leaving early at the age of 16 after winning the equivalent of a quarter of a million pounds from an accumulator horse race bet. "A man of my means should not remain a schoolboy," he reputedly announced at a celebration boarding house dinner.

Zac too left Eton early, also aged 16, though the circumstances of his departure were less triumphant. He was, to use the diplomatic language, invited to leave after cannabis was found in his room. That mishap was in 1991. In the same year, Khan completed his law degree then went on to do his Law Society finals at the College of Law in Guildford in Surrey. Goldsmith, picking up the pieces, moved on to another fee-paying school, the Cambridge Centre for Sixth Form Studies. He emerged with four A-levels but did not go on to university. Instead, he travelled the world: Mexico, New Zealand, Hungary, Italy, Thailand and more. His patron was his father's elder brother Edward.

"Teddy" Goldsmith, like Sir James, was energetic and flamboyant but his passions were utterly different. Sir James was a gambler, a philanderer and a voracious capitalist, derided as an asset-stripper. Teddy was a radical environmentalist, an enemy of industrialism and a defender of cultures threatened by it. He feared the Earth was dying. In 1970 he founded a magazine called the Ecologist. The year Sir James died, Edward made Zac its reviews editor. The following year the young Goldsmith stepped up to become editor-in-chief.

He did this work unpaid, but he got by. He entered the new millennium newly married, impossibly rich and keen to save the world. A Daily Telegraph feature from 2000 describes a cheerfully chaotic 25-year-old smoking organic cigarettes in a Chelsea Wharf office containing a sleeping Labrador, unwashed mugs and an overflowing bin. He was preparing to open an organic restaurant, the only type he wished to eat in, what with so many pigs full of cancer. He was about to re-launch the magazine to make it less academic and more fun. An activist called Agent Apple would talk about shoving cream pies in the faces of people he considered to be harming the planet.

Goldsmith's wife, whom he'd wed the previous June, was nine months pregnant. Sheherazade Bentley was the daughter of noted 1970s corporate predator John Bentley and Colombian actress Viviane Ventura who had written a book on the art of social climbing. Fertility, it seemed, was not an issue for Goldsmith himself, though in this he considered himself fortunate. "Every man today is afraid he's firing blanks," he explained. He'd been reading some Danish research: "We now have the sperm count of a hamster."

*****

Meanwhile, in another part of town, Sadiq Khan had become a Labour councillor in his home borough of Wandsworth - a noted Conservative

stronghold - and later a partner in the law firm
Christian Khan. While Goldsmith was revamping the
Ecologist, Khan was representing eleven Kurdish
refugees who'd sued the Metropolitan Police for
damages. Four years earlier, the refugees had
been rehearsing the Harold Pinter play Mountain
Language, a work about state oppression of Kurds
in Turkey, at a community centre in Haringey. One
scene had involved some of the actors dressed in
combat gear pointing guns at others sitting on the
floor.

Somebody, confusing art with life, had
dialled 999. Officers smashed down the doors. A
police helicopter circled above. The actors were
handcuffed, thrown in a van and forbidden to
speak in their native tongue. The Met declined
to accept liability for the trauma some of their
captives claimed they'd experienced as a result, but
Khan secured the Kurds a pay out.

In 2001 he made the news again when
controversial black American political campaigner
Louis Farrakhan, leader of the Nation of Islam,
won a High Court case to overturn the Labour
government's maintaining a long-standing ban on
him visiting the UK. The Home Secretary argued
that Farrakhan had voiced "anti-Semitic and
racially divisive views". But Khan, representing the
Nation of Islam, told the BBC the judicial decision
was "very brave and sensible". He said of Farrakhan
that there was "no evidence at all that any of his

other trips to countries around the world, including Israel, had led to any problems whatsoever".

The government appealed and won. Once more, though, Khan defended his client to the BBC. "He is preaching a message of self-discipline, self-reliance, atonement and responsibility," he said of Farrakhan: "He's trying to address the issues and problems we have in the UK – black on black crime and problems in the black community."

Khan's profile as a lawyer grew. In November 2003, a police officer client, Chief Inspector Leroy Logan, was awarded a six-figure sum in compensation after being cleared of falsely claiming £80 in expenses for a hotel bill. The Met had dug into Logan's affairs as part of an inquiry into another of Khan's clients at that time, a more senior Met officer, Superintendent Ali Dizaei.

The long story of Dizaei's disputes with the Met eventually ended in 2013, when he lost an appeal against convictions for misconduct in public office and perverting the course of justice. But in September 2003, when Khan was his solicitor, an Old Bailey jury acquitted him of misconduct. Other charges against him were dropped. He received £80,000 in compensation and was later promoted.

Logan chaired the Metropolitan Black Police Association, which represents the interests of ethnic minority officers, and had been awarded an MBE for his contribution to developing anti-racist policing policies. He'd brought an employment tribunal case against his employer, claiming racial discrimination and victimisation. The Met settled just before the case was due to start.

During this period, Khan chaired the civil liberties pressure group Liberty. But his star was rising in the political world too. Earlier in 2003 he had been selected to be Labour candidate for his home constituency of Tooting at the next general election. Two years later he retained the seat for his party. That was on 5 May 2005. On 7 July that year, four young British Muslims killed themselves and 52 other people by detonating bombs on London public transport during the morning rush hour. The atrocity became known as the London Bombings or 7/7.

In parliament, the newcomer Khan made a number of contributions to the ensuing debate about Britain's response to Islamism. He was one of the Labour MPs who helped defeat the plan of the Labour government led by Tony Blair to hold terrorism suspects for 90 days without charge. All of this made a good impression on the panel that awarded the 2005 Parliamentarian of the Year awards for the Spectator magazine, a weekly journal from the right of the political spectrum. Khan was named Newcomer of the Year. The citation said:

> "The judges were unanimous in singling out this MP for the tough-mindedness and clarity with which he has spoken about the

very difficult issues of Islamic terror. Some cited a certain theatricality in his voice, with one judge calling it a 'strong, physical voice'. Others praised his energy, likening him to a steel spring, a rubber band or a coiled leopard. But the award mainly reflects the eloquence and ability with which he has represented a part of society that is in need of cogent representation."

The florid language used for describing Khan was characteristic of Boris Johnson, the Spectator's editor at that time as well as being the MP for Henley in Oxfordshire. Three years later Johnson, an Old Etonian like Goldsmith, won the first of his two terms as London Mayor. It was he whom Khan and Goldsmith would later vie to succeed in the role.

*****

In career terms, Zac Goldsmith's first five years of the new millennium centred on the Ecologist. His signed editorial in the April 2000 re-launch issue was headlined "Beware Politicians Bearing Gifts". Goldsmith railed against the failure of Western powers to relieve the nations of the poor South of their debts. Tony Blair and United States President Bill Clinton had publicly supported a campaign to do so, and yet very little had changed. Goldsmith wondered if the left-wing journalist John Pilger was right to suggest that "some of the most poisonous forces to have shaped the latter half of the previous century have carried off a 'propaganda triumph' that will propagate their activities throughout the current century?" Goldsmith concluded: "It is time not only that we 'forgive' the developing world its debts, but that we clear our own debts with them."

The light of Goldsmith's zeal kept shining bright. He described spending six months in the Ladakh region of the Himalayas as "probably the most interesting time in my life". Here was a society "that worked in many ways better than our own. It embraced place, there was no homelessness, there were no basic needs not being met." He described the political establishment's case that the world's poorer countries should be given the chance to narrow the development gap with the rich ones as "a fundamental lie" which would, in any case, be ruinous: "The Earth cannot sustain the process of Third World countries catching up with us." He despaired of global capitalism and the political system: "People are lost. There's not a huge amount of choice now. They are unhooking themselves from the political system, disentangling themselves from party politics. It's not apathy. They feel that the vote just does not count."

What was the answer? "How many people actually live ecologically?" he asked: "You just can't.

If you live in a great dirty city, you cannot help live a dirty life." But perhaps it could be found in Rajasthan, where villages had joined together to re-assert their self-sufficiency: "It was a desert [there], dependent utterly on the state and international aid agencies. Then they threw a metaphorical wall around their villages, brought back traditional agriculture, making their own medicines, starting their own schools. They've created a jungle out of the desert. The water table has risen. They have no GDP, but their own currency. They have enriched their own lives enormously." Goldsmith's quest was bold, but he was driven to achieve it: "I'm not going to be happy until there is complete change in the world. I know I have to do it."

Goldsmith smoked roll-ups and re-cycled, notably by wearing some of his father's old suits. He gave money to organisations opposed to genetically modified crops, nuclear power and industrial farming methods. He bought Walreddon Manor, a 534-acre estate at the edge of Dartmoor, near Tavistock in Devon, a county he would later describe as "the most authentic part of rural England, with its villages, small farms and market towns". At Walreddon, he planted "hundreds of thousands of native trees" and raised organic livestock, albeit with the help of a tenant and kindly neighbours, one of whom once remarked to him that as "a Jewish pig farmer" Goldsmith was probably unique.

Goldsmith, in fact, has said he "cannot claim to be all that Jewish", although his paternal grandfather, originally named Franck Goldschmidt, was a Jew from Frankfurt who'd moved permanently to Britain as a teenager at the back end of the 19th century. He'd Anglicised his family name and gone on to become a British army officer and a Conservative MP in Suffolk until after the outbreak of Word World I when his German origins were discovered, riots broke out and he left England in disillusion before becoming a successful hotelier in France.

His grandson Zac sank a lot of cash into the Ecologist. Under his editorship, the magazine's circulation trebled to around 20,000 copies a month. It ran accusatory front pages: Dying for DeBeers; Eat Shit Or Die. Goldsmith's editorials took a strongly anti-globalisation line. "Like most governments, ours believes the interests of the multi nationals are one and the same as the interests of ordinary people," he wrote in 2003. As Goldsmith saw it, while corporate big cheeses were free to do as they pleased, small cheese-makers in Devon were being crushed.

The dissident young Goldsmith was pro-small business and small communities, localist and conservationist. He was against overbearing government from whatever source, including the European Union as his father had famously been – Sir James had even formed his own Referendum Party to campaign for a national vote on whether

24

Britain should remain an EU member. From such planks his philosophical platform was constructed. In 2005, the year Sadiq Khan was first elected to parliament, Goldsmith decided to expand on to a new stage - he joined the Conservative Party.

*****

The future mayoral antagonists now moved up the ranks of their respective parties. Goldsmith began ascending first. The Tories lost the 2005 general election. It was their third defeat in a row. In December of that year, the party chose a new leader. David Cameron, yet another Old Etonian, was young, personable, skilled at presentation and determined to rebrand the Tories - thought of by many voters as "the Nasty Party" according to the then future Home Secretary Theresa May - as inclusive, caring and green. He embarked on a major overhaul of policy. At the London Wetland Centre by Barnes Common in the suburban south-west London borough of Richmond upon Thames, he met members of Friends of the Earth and Greenpeace and unveiled his environment team, instructed to explore climate change and quality of life themes.

Zac Goldsmith, a local man, was the team's vice-chairman. He was still a roll-up smoker and still maintained that he was "cynical about politicians".

But he thought the new Tory leader an exception to the rule. "I don't know David Cameron very well," Goldsmith said of his fellow Eton alumnus. However: "I like him. I think you can judge a book by its cover...that's the whole point of nature giving us intuition, instinct and so. I think the cover is pretty good." He said he'd chosen to back the Tories because, in his view, Labour had become "the party of big business". Cameron seemed to like Goldsmith too. Certainly, he liked what he believed Goldsmith could do for the Conservatives. He assembled an "A-list" of new candidates to fight seats at the next general election to personify the new model Tories: young, diverse and "with it" as people from Cameron's background possibly still say.

Goldsmith was on the list. He was lined up for the safe parliamentary seat of East Hampshire, but dropped out at the eleventh hour. "I just didn't know about East Hampshire," he later explained. He'd written articles complaining that politicians were too often parachuted in to areas with which they had no connection. "The whole thing was so artificial," he explained: "I had a panic and I wrote to them telling them I couldn't do it." He was more comfortable entering an open primary held by the Conservative Association of Richmond Park and North Kingston, where he lived. He won.

As Goldsmith moved towards challenging for a parliamentary seat, Khan continued to advance the arguments about his fellow British Muslims and Islamist terror for which Boris Johnson and his colleagues at the Spectator had given him a prize. In 2006, he was a signatory to a letter published in the Guardian from prominent Muslim groups and individuals which argued that the Labour government should not ignore "the role of its foreign policy" including the "debacle of Iraq" in increasing the risk to ordinary people in the Middle East and providing "ammunition to extremists who threaten us all".

But from June 2007, when Gordon Brown became Labour prime minister after Tony Blair stepped down, Khan began moving up the parliamentary ranks. Brown made him a government whip, responsible for ensuring that MPs got legislation through the Commons. In July 2008, Khan helped to push through a 42-day version of the controversial detention plan he had helped vote down three years earlier. The director of Liberty, Shami Chakrabarti was among those who were deeply critical. His principles were called into question. Some recalled that he had left his law firm Christian Khan rather abruptly upon winning his parliamentary seat.

Brown, though, thought highly of Khan. Three months later, he made him minister for communities. Also in 2008, Khan published a pamphlet for the Fabian Society, Britain's oldest political think tank and a Labour affiliate. Khan was

chair of the Fabians at the time. Entitled Fairness
not Favours, his pamphlet argued that Labour
needed to reconnect with British Muslims, many of
whom had become disillusioned with the party as
a result of Blair's decision to take Britain into the
war against Iraq.

Criticising what he called a "lazy" engagement
with community leaders by politicians Khan
advocated "a real, open and honest relationship
with a wide spectrum of Muslim individuals and
groups". But he added: "This is a relationship of
two sides. British Muslims also need to step up to
the plate. We need to take responsibility for our
own lives. We need to take more responsibility
for our own families, ignore those who propagate
conspiracy theories and, above all, we need to
leave behind our victim mentality." Khan worked in
the Department for Communities for eight months
before Brown transferred him to the Department
for Transport, where he was again minister of state.
In this role, he became the first Muslim to attend
cabinet. That political high point was maintained
into the early months of 2010. Then came another
general election.

Zac Goldsmith had formally become the
Conservative candidate for Richmond Park and
North Kingston. He had also become divorced: his
split with Sheherazade, with whom he'd had three
children, excited gossip columns with talk of record-
breaking financial settlements. Richmond Park was

represented by Liberal Democrat Susan Kramer, a prominent member of her party who had run for London Mayor in 2000. Goldsmith took the seat from her with a 7% swing and entered parliament for the first time. But though his was one of many gains his party made across the country, there weren't enough of them to secure a Tory majority. David Cameron had to form a coalition with the Lib Dems in order to enter 10 Downing Street. A big reason for that was that the Conservatives did less well in London than they'd hoped to. One of the seats they'd targeted was Khan's. Instead, he strengthened his hold with a 3.6% swing away from the Tory runner-up.

*****

And so the two men who would later battle each other for City Hall took seats in parliament together for the first time. Both made marks on their parties' futures. After the defeated Gordon Brown stepped down as Labour leader, Khan organised the successful campaign of erstwhile Environment Secretary Ed Miliband to replace him. Against expectations, Miliband prevailed over his elder brother David by a tiny margin. Goldsmith's preoccupation was local and environmental. His seat is under the flight path of Heathrow airport, Britain's largest. Debate had raged for years about whether expanding it was the best way to increase Britain's air transport capacity. Goldsmith was strongly against.

In 2009, David Cameron had felt the same way. As leader of Her Majesty's Opposition he ruled out expanding Heathrow. "No ifs, no buts," he said. The Labour government of that time and transport minister Khan had been in favour. But, in 2012, Prime Minister Cameron set up a commission to look at the whole issue afresh. Goldsmith was unhappy. He said he would not stand as a Conservative at the next general election if his party went into it favouring adding a third runway at Heathrow after all. In April 2013, returning to the Wetland Centre where he'd publically joined with Cameron seven years before, he addressed a rally. "No ifs, no buts, we will stop Heathrow expansion," he declared.

By then, Ed Miliband's Labour had blurred its Heathrow stance and Khan had become shadow Justice Secretary. It was not his only job for the new boss whose elevation to that position he'd helped bring about. At the start of 2013 Miliband had appointed him shadow London minister as well. Khan's immediate task was to co-ordinate Labour's campaign effort for elections to the capital's 32 borough councils and the European parliament in May 2014. The year after that would come the next general election, when he would again marshal Labour's resources in the capital.

But all the background talk was of him lining up a 2016 mayoral bid.

Privately, he did not deny it. Sometimes, he would elaborate. The difficult choice between becoming London Mayor and being Justice Secretary in a Labour government would be made easier depending on the size of any Miliband victory: a clear one would make a second term more likely and a lot could be achieved in ten years; a single term would, by contrast, be limiting. The more slender any general election win, therefore, the greater the rival attractions of the mayoralty. It followed, of course, that a Miliband defeat would resolve the dilemma instantly. In December 2013, Khan edited a collection of essays for the Fabians entitled Our London. The signal was unmistakable.

Tories too were pondering the future. Mayor Johnson had made clear that his second term at City Hall, secured in 2102, would be his last. With him, all speculation concerned his barely concealed designs on Cameron's job and when he would take the vital step towards seizing it of securing a return to the Commons. Johnson is a unique figure in British politics, an unprecedented blend of comedian, conman, *faux* subversive showman and populist media confection. These qualities fitted him superbly for the figurehead aspects of being mayor. His was a dazzling act. What Tory could hope to follow the performance known as "Boris"?

Celebrities from other fields were auditioned in the press, but none took the cue to walk on stage. Only one eligible politician seemed to possess anything like the qualities convention deemed essential in a mayoral candidate: charisma and a readiness to break party rank. Only Goldsmith passed these tests. Yet he had only recently ruled out a mayoral bid. He said he didn't fancy his chances of winning, adding: "I think people have had enough of white male Etonians. It's simply not going to happen. I'm not going to stand as candidate for Mayor of London."

In May 2014, Labour made gains in the metropolis, taking the number of boroughs they controlled up to 20 out of 32. Khan went on deflecting questions about the mayoralty. Other Labour politicians made known their interest in running for mayor, but as the 2015 general election approached, Khan dodged on: he reasoned that he had a Labour Prime Minister to help deliver and would not place himself in the position of appearing to be distracted from that task. With no Cameron commitment on Heathrow either way, Goldsmith made ready to defend Richmond Park as a Conservative. Reckoning day drew near and opinion polls pointed to a Miliband-led hung parliament. They turned out to be completely wrong. Cameron won a small but unforeseen majority. The man Khan had helped to become

Labour leader was defeated, miserably. He stepped down immediately.

Results in London, though, did not fit the national pattern. Labour picked up seven seats, almost as many as predicted, lifting its total to 45 out of 73. It took a 43.7% share of the total London vote compared with the Conservatives' 34.9%. Khan retained his Tooting seat by a slightly increased majority. Yet although they lost ground to Labour in London, there were consolations for the Tories: their vote share was fractionally up on 2010 and their seats score fell only by one, to 27. Like Labour, they made gains at the expense of a beleaguered Lib Dems. And Goldsmith, by then remarried to banking heiress Alice Rothschild and a father of four, not only held on to Richmond Park, he did so resoundingly, increasing his majority by a massive 18,924 votes.

These outcomes strengthened the arguments for both men to seek the mayoralty the following year. Khan would have liked a larger victory in Tooting, but the overall London outcome could hardly reflect badly on him. Miliband's undoing had, in any case, cemented his decision to set his sights on City Hall. As for Goldsmith, his formidable parliamentary mandate, albeit owing much to the implosion of the Lib Dems which had reduced them to just a single London seat, had the look of a huge personal endorsement. London's mayors are directly elected. If Richmond Park Londoners had taken him to their hearts, might not other Londoners do the same?

Voters' impressions of politicians as people matters in all high profile elections, but in London mayoral campaigns it can matter – and be portrayed as mattering – that bit more. If Goldsmith himself was still undecided about entering the contest at that stage, evidence arguing that he was the strongest potential candidate had become overwhelming. What was more, his party needed him. As that Parliament Square meeting with Khan later showed, he would answer its call.

Two

Selection

Labour had been the first of the two big political parties to set about selecting its candidate. Its London activists and politicians, still groggy from Ed Miliband's shattering defeat, were back on their feet and game for further punishment within days. Khan resigned from the shadow cabinet. By 13 May, six contenders had stepped into the ring: Diane Abbott, a veteran left-wing MP for poor but gentrifying inner city Hackney North and Stoke Newington; seasoned author and transport commentator Christian Wolmar, a resident of Islington who'd never fought any kind of election before; Gareth Thomas, the MP for suburban Harrow West and a leading light of Labour affiliate the Co-operative Party; Tottenham MP David Lammy, who represents one of London's most deprived constituencies; and, completing the line-up with Khan, his fellow former minister Tessa Jowell, who'd stepped down as MP for Dulwich and West Norwood before the general election.

Jowell was expected to win. Her credentials were impressive. A London MP for 23 years and before that a Camden councillor, she had been Culture Secretary under Tony Blair and, in that capacity, talked him into supporting London's bid to host the 2012 Olympics. As Olympics minister, she was central to the project's progress. Although out of office by the time the Games took place, much of the credit for their success attached to her. Jowell could justly claim that she knew how to make things happen in the capital. She was also that unusual thing, a genuinely well-liked politician. Bookmakers and opinion polls made her the favourite to become the next mayor.

But Khan too had strong factors in his favour, among them the selection process itself. Lammy had long called for an open primary to pick the candidate, which would have allowed any adult Londoner at all to cast a vote. In the event, and after various adjustments, a far more closed system had been settled on. The Labour "selectorate" would comprise London party members, London members of those trade unions and other organisations affiliated to Labour, and other members of the public who paid £3 to become "registered supporters".

The inclusion of union members was thought likely to assist candidates from the left. Khan was not the leftmost one. He was from the "soft left" of the party mainstream. Both the outsider Wolmar and the high profile Abbott were further out on that wing. Khan had, though, been courting union support. When Labour's National Executive Committee decided to change the date for the mayoral decision, moving it back from the end of July to September when the party's new leader would also be announced, there were mutterings that this allowed more time for union members to sign up, to the disadvantage of Thomas, Lammy and Jowell.

It was, though, harder to quarrel with the scale and breadth of support Khan attracted from fellow London politicians. Within a week of the line-up of runners being settled Khan was posing for photographs outside City Hall with two of the most influential endorsers he could have wished for.

One was Ken Livingstone, the very first holder of the post of London Mayor and a giant figure in London government for more than 30 years. "Red Ken" as he became known when he was the final leader of the old Greater London Council in the 1980s had, following an unremarkable spell as an MP, made a spectacular political comeback in 2000 by winning the mayoralty as an independent after London Labour members, fervently encouraged by Blair, had not chosen him as their candidate.

In his first four-year term, Livingstone demonstrated the blend of imagination, conviction and pragmatism that had marked him out from other figures on the Outer Left to revolutionise the capital's bus service, create a road traffic congestion charging zone, get the Metropolitan

Police to introduce community policing and fight Gordon Brown, then the Labour Chancellor of the Exchequer, over the financing of the long overdue modernisation of the London Underground. In 2004, by then readmitted to Labour, which had expelled him for his earlier defiance, Livingstone won a second term. Despite their deep political differences, he had worked closely with Jowell to bring the Olympics to London and had impressed with his response to the 7/7 bombings, which took place the day after the momentous announcement that the Games bid had been successful.

Knowledgeable almost to a fault about the workings of London municipal government, Livingstone had successfully converted the mayoral blueprint into a functioning, formidable reality, just as he had transformed his own public image from that of "the most odious man in Britain" according to the Sun newspaper into that of a charmingly irascible rogue and, until Johnson came along, the only politician in Britain usually referred to by his first name alone. The combative and sometimes scathing style of the unlikely celebrity known as "Ken" ensured that he made enemies inside his own party. Yet despite this and his successive defeats by Johnson in 2008 and, most gallingly, in 2012 when Labour in London was otherwise on the rise, the veteran, archetypal London leftie remained a big star in the capital's political firmament.

The backing of Livingstone was still more valuable to Khan for being counterbalanced by a significant figure from a very different part of Labour's broad and often quarrelsome church. Four years earlier, Oona King, formerly MP for the East End constituency of Bethnal Green and Bow, had been the sole Labour challenger to Livingstone when he'd sought the mayoral nomination for his ill-fated rematch with Johnson in the Olympics year. She'd been decisively beaten, but Livingstone's description of her as an "uber Blairite" had captured much of her value to Khan. Her commendation meant he could claim support from all wings of the party. In addition, King was of Khan's younger generation, female and of mixed ethnicity. Between them, she and Livingstone covered London Labour's symbolism waterfront.

To get on the selection ballot paper, each of the hopefuls had first to secure five or more nominations from Labour's 73 parliamentary constituency parties. Each CLP could nominate two of the six, at least one of which had to be a woman. This obviously helped Jowell and Abbott against the four men, although, given that the former was famously Blairite and the latter a long-term critic of the now former Prime Minister, this arrangement effectively threw them into a separate contest with each other, since no CLP was likely to pick them both. Jowell's massive 63 nominations compared with Abbott's eight was therefore not necessarily quite as huge an endorsement as it appeared. But it was still formidable. The men's race was always going to be closer, but Khan still won it comfortably. He received 44 nominations to Lammy's 15 and the six apiece of Thomas and Wolmar.

In mid-June, after interviews with a panel of NEC and London region members, the full half dozen went forward to the starting line. In terms of background, sex, ethnicity, power base, area represented and position on Labour's ideological spectrum, the field could not have been more diverse. In terms of victory prospects, Khan and Jowell looked to be out in front. Khan had already secured the backing of 14 of London's 45 Labour MPs, more than any other candidate, plus a large pack of Labour councillors. The GMB and Unite unions were behind him too.

Meanwhile, Labour's leadership contest formally began in parallel. Its smaller field of four only reached that number because of a last-minute addition. Jeremy Corbyn, the MP for Islington North, was very few Labour MPs' idea of a suitable leader. But a bunch of them decided to "lend" him their nomination vote. Corbyn secured the number of these he needed just minutes before the noon deadline on 15 June. One of those who helped him was Khan. Those who'd bestowed their largesse in this way spoke charitably of broadening the debate. But Corbyn's presence in the leadership contest would have a far larger impact than Khan or any of the other MPs who'd nominated him could have imagined at the time.

*****

At first, the mayoral selection race was the more interesting and also the more fruitful of the two Labour internal contests as the six candidates set out an array of approaches and ideas. In some respects Lammy was the best prepared. Before becoming Tottenham's MP he had very briefly been a member of the 25-strong London Assembly, the elected body which scrutinises the London Mayor. He had long coveted the City Hall job and only drawn back from a bid to run for Labour in 2012 after accepting that he couldn't stop Livingstone from making his comeback attempt.

Irked by his belief that Khan had been given an inside track under his ally Ed Miliband, Lammy had formally launched his campaign for 2016 in September 2014. He'd rebranded himself with new suits and contact lenses in place of spectacles and released an impressive document on housing policy, a burgeoning London issue.

He was not, though, the first to have declared. Wolmar had announced his candidacy way back in autumn September 2012, expressing dissatisfaction with the previous spring's campaigns by both the victorious Johnson and the again defeated

Livingstone. He'd been engaged in a grassroots charm offensive ever since, speaking to almost 80 meetings, traversing the capital on his bicycle. Abbott and Jowell had signalled their interest more obliquely, declaring their intentions to declare at a later date. Thomas had dropped his hint as recently as February. With Khan at last out in the open, the flirting phase was over. More serious advances could now begin.

The first hustings was held without delay on the evening of 16 June at the grand Emmanuel conference centre on Marsham Street in Westminster. The venue was significant for being the original home of the London Assembly, before City Hall was built. The independent Mayor Livingstone and the Greater London Authority, the administrative body which serves the mayor and the assembly, had been installed along the road in Romney House.

The co-hosts of the hustings were think tank Centre for London and Prospect magazine, kindred spirits in devout non-alignment. An opening show of hands confirmed that Jowell was the audience's favourite. She played directly to her strengths, pointing out that Labour had not won a major election for ten years or a mayoral one for eleven: "Let's be clear. In this election Labour needs a candidate who can win and London needs a candidate who can deliver." As well as the Olympics, she cited the Sure Start programme for pre-school children she'd introduced when a public health minster as a major achievement. "I know how to get things done and I know how to bring people together. I have the vision and I have the plans to build One London," she said, introducing a touchstone phrase.

A key task for campaigning politicians is to define and highlight differences from their main opponent. Jowell spoke of young entrepreneurs needing help to put their ideas into effect. Khan too stressed London as a place where ambition should be nurtured. He, though, could personalise the point: "If you work hard, your potential can be fulfilled, whether you were born here or if you chose to come here, as my parents did." The foundations for this success were, in Khan's case, laid by the state: "Good, decent council accommodation. Good, decent jobs. Good, decent schools." He wasn't having Jowell laying sole claim to winnability: "What we need is a candidate who's going to win, from Bromley to Balham, from Redbridge to Richmond. Winning is crucial." Then came his differential sign-off: "Winning for a purpose." The insinuation was that Jowell was the continuity candidate, who as mayor would be little different from Boris Johnson. He, by contrast, was for change. The stress on his London background was no accident either: Jowell, the daughter of medical professionals, had been educated at an independent school in Aberdeen.

Working class roots still carry weight in the Labour Party. Of the other candidates, only Lammy could compete with Khan's life story. Born and raised in Tottenham to Guyanese parents, he, his mother and his four siblings were abandoned by their father when Lammy was twelve. They struggled to get by and, as Lammy made sure to point out, lived a few hundred yards from the Broadwater Farm estate, a place forever synonymous with a notorious riot in 1985 that left a police officer dead. A barrister who'd worked as a security guard and for Kentucky Fried Chicken, Lammy too could speak with authority about childhood support from the public sector in the form of teachers and youth workers fostering social mobility. As a ten year-old he'd won a scholarship from the (later abolished) Inner London Education Authority to attend the celebrated King's School in Peterborough and be a chorister at Peterborough cathedral. He'd later been awarded a first class law degree and become the first black Briton to study the subject at Harvard.

Politically, though, he and Khan were of different weaves. Lammy had been a junior minister for five years under Blair, but not prospered as some had hoped. He'd since recast himself as an independent voice, potentially able to appeal to London voters normally beyond the reach of Labour politicians. He had won praise for his response to the London Riots of 2011, which began in Tottenham after armed officers shot dead a young man, Mark Duggan. In Out of the Ashes, a book springing from that experience, Lammy had expounded a philosophy blaming a combination of free market economics and liberal orthodoxies for a collapse in social solidarity that hurt the disadvantaged most. He saw Khan as a party insider, a position that meant the balance between principle and pragmatism might not be quite right. If a third participant was to threaten the front two, it seemed likely to be Lammy at this stage.

Inequality, opportunity and authenticity were always going to be bedrock factors in the Labour candidacy race, yet the debate reached into wider territory. Wolmar, who despite his inexperience did not look out of his depth at Emmanuel House, gave a prominence to the connections between London's transport systems and the poor quality of its air that the debate would otherwise have lacked. Abbott, another to depict herself as a free spirit, offered good-humoured hard left didacticism. But the most original vision from an unfancied runner was Thomas's. Not one hand was raised in his favour as proceedings got underway. He was not deterred: "At the heart of my campaign are two simple premises: firstly, that more power should be devolved to London; secondly, that more power should be devolved to Londoners." Thomas argued that with Scotland, Wales and Northern Ireland all securing greater autonomy, a federal Britain was taking shape and that London should be "treated as a city state" within the United Kingdom.

The label was more provocative than the content: all candidates advocated the devolution of property taxes to the capital, as had been recommended in a report compiled for Johnson. But Thomas's terminology reclaimed as a virtue the commonplace charge that London had become too big and dominant, a gluttonous parasite engorged by the lifeblood of the rest of the country. And he lengthened the devolution wish list to include giving the mayor power to regulate private sector rents and set a statutory London minimum wage. He also suggested measures to further fertilise the capital's economic growth that none of his rivals would risk, even if they subscribed to them.

One of these concerned aviation capacity. Mayor Johnson's contribution to the decades-long debate about the issue had been to revive and hyper-inflate an old idea of locating a brand new airport in the Thames Estuary. Various iterations of a spectacular "Boris Island" hub had entertained the press for years, notwithstanding London's mayors having not the slightest power to sanction such an enterprise. The commission set up by David Cameron had dumped that idea in September 2014, but the views of Johnson's aspiring successors on airport capacity were still sought and thought important.

Expansion options had boiled down to adding a third runway at Heathrow or a second one at Gatwick airport, south of Greater London in West Sussex. For Thomas, there was no choice to be made between the two – he wanted one at each. None of his Labour colleagues were going to fly that high. Both Jowell and Lammy were for expanding Heathrow. But although Khan had been so when a transport minister, on the day of the hustings he told the Evening Standard, the sole London newspaper distributed throughout the whole of the metropolis, of his opposition to it and his preference for augmenting Gatwick instead. He gave air quality and noise pollution as his reasons, though the political advantages seem unlikely to have escaped him. Backing Heathrow was a potential vote-loser. Whatever its blend of idealism and compromise, Khan's route to the candidacy would not want for electoral calculus.

*****

Zac Goldsmith had less need than Khan for positional refinements. For months he had been touted as the Conservative politician best equipped for the job of succeeding Mayor Johnson. He was his party's up-river crown prince. Had he failed to the secure the nomination it would have been sensational. Interest in the Tory selection contest therefore lay largely in how he shaped up as the party's City Hall challenger in waiting.

His first move was to announce that he would seek the blessing of his Richmond Park constituents before formally joining the candidate race. Postal ballots were sent to all 77,000 of them, complete with pre-paid envelopes for their return. Around a quarter responded, taking the cost of the exercise to Goldsmith to close to £50,000. A large majority gave their consent. On 23 June Goldsmith said he was "hugely grateful" to them, assiduously praised Johnson as "a strong campaigning mayor" on whose watch "London has become the world's greatest city" and officially stepped into the fray to become his successor. One bookmaker made him 2/1 favourite to prevail.

Placing his political future in the hands of his constituents was in keeping with Goldsmith's enthusiasm for what is called "direct democracy", whereby voters are given the power to decide on specific policy matters through referenda rather than leaving it to their elected representatives. He holds that MPs should be subject to the power of recall between elections if enough constituents want them removed. Goldsmith's belief in enhancing politicians' accountability in this way was thereby signalled as one he would live by. He was effectively saying: "As mayor, I would serve Londoners, not myself."

The following month, he gave an interview to LBC Radio. The government's airports commission had just published its final report, recommending that a third runway should be built at Heathrow. Goldsmith had already said he believed commission chair, the former businessman Sir Howard Davies, had made his mind up on the issue before the three-year study had even begun. Sir Howard's stinging response was that Goldsmith had "no privileged access to my thought processes" and must therefore be "lying".

Presenter Iain Dale probed. Did Goldsmith owe Sir Howard an apology? "Absolutely not," Goldsmith replied. He said he'd supplied the commission with important information, including from Transport for London, whose job is to implement mayoral transport policy, about the additional road capacity that would be needed if a third runway was built, but that Davies hadn't even acknowledged receipt. "My opinion, it's not a fact, but my view is that Sir Howard Davies began with a conclusion, he didn't deviate, and £20m later he ended up in exactly the same place that he'd intended to end up," Goldsmith said.

He said that expanding Heathrow, which is owned by a consortium including Chinese, Singaporean and Qatari government funds and Spanish and Canadian businesses, would be bad for competition with other airports and that "effectively what we're being asked to do is channel huge amounts of taxpayer subsidy into creating a vast, foreign-owned monopoly". He also expressed complete confidence that, notwithstanding the findings of the Davies commission, the government would rule against Heathrow expansion before the end of the year: "I couldn't be more confident of that."

Even so, he confirmed that if the government did eventually agree with Davies he would keep his long-standing promise to resign as an MP and so trigger a by-election in Richmond Park. He would not, though, contest that by-election. That would be because he would continue running for mayor, and he couldn't do that and fight a parliamentary by-election at the same time. He would also continue to be the Tory mayoral candidate. "A mayoral campaign is not just about Richmond Park and North Kingston, nor is it just about Heathrow," he reasoned.

LBC shows are webcast. In his body language as in his speech, Goldsmith conveyed a blend of stubbornness and diffidence that some found puzzling, others beguiling. His eyes frequently dropped and slid away as he spoke, even though his speech was confident and fluent. He was asked about a protest that had taken place at Heathrow, causing disruption to passengers. It was "unfortunate," he said, that this had "put customers, people, out more than anyone else. Any protest that puts the public's nose out of joint is going to be counterproductive". Protest had to be about winning arguments: "I don't think you win the arguments if you alienate huge numbers of people."

Dale asked him why he'd left Eton. "Do I have so say this on the radio?" Goldsmith asked with a hint of a squirm and a blush. He owned up: "Cannabis was found in my room. I was guilty throughout my time at school, but on this one occasion I was innocent. But it seemed pointless at the time to put up any resistance. I learned my lesson, I think you could say."

"Do you regard yourself as a rebel?" Dale asked.

"No, not really," Goldsmith replied: "I'm independent-minded." He felt this was essential if you were to represent the people who elected you, rather than being a compliant party hack. "That occasionally has made me a pain in the backside in parliament," he said: "On the big issues it hasn't, but it has enabled me to hold government to account on issues I think are important on behalf of my constituents."

Would a Mayor Goldsmith be a pain in Prime Minister Cameron's backside, as some had claimed?

"I don't think it's true at all. But it's not about the Tory party. It's about London. If the contest is all about advancing the interests of one party over another, then it's not a very interesting enterprise and London will invariably lose out. I work very closely with David Cameron on a range of issues.

I get along very well with him. He knows that if there's a policy I don't support, I will stand my ground. I don't think it suits anyone's interest to have an MP or a councillor or a mayor who submits themselves to a kind of voluntary lobotomy simply to vote the party line."

Dale put it to him that if he became the Tory candidate, Labour would be sure to mock him as a toff who didn't know what ordinary life was like. Goldsmith described learning important lessons from a disabled constituent: "You don't need to be dependent on a wheelchair in order to understand how important it is to have access to our Tube and train stations. The key issue is empathy and an ability to solve problems."

He was asked what Boris Johnson's greatest failure had been. He declined to point one out. He'd earlier described Johnson as a "great mayor".

*****

The Labour candidate sextet roamed the capital throughout the summer. A sweltering hustings at the University of Westminster organised by the London Labour Housing Group underlined that housing was becoming the hottest topic in town. A distinctive Lammy proposal was to raise money from the bond markets to build social housing, an aspiration that expressed the working-class traditionalist part of his pitch. Jowell was booed for saying, quite correctly, that rough sleeping was a complex mental health issue as well as a housing one. She had some populist lines too, though: higher council tax for foreign investors in homes who don't live in them or let them. Khan wanted a clamp down on overseas investors too. In this, both spoke to a belief, fostered by journalists and reflected in polls, that rich foreigners were the number one cause of house price inflation in London, which was running at more than 10% a year.

Khan proposed introducing a "London living rent" tenure, whereby private sector rents would be linked to average local earnings. Both he and Jowell argued that the next mayor should set up a not-for-profit lettings agency to undercut commercial operators, often accused of overcharging tenants and landlords alike - a policy Livingstone had offered, in consultation with Jowell, in 2012. Both said they would set up a unit called Homes for Londoners, which would help drive the supply of the homes the city needed most. They vied to be the one who would install this unit nearest to their desk.

At this stage in the long selection slog, Jowell looked to be ascendant. A poll had found that she would comfortably beat Goldsmith in an actual mayoral election, while Khan would only tie with him. Jowell had also received the influential endorsement of Len Duvall, leader of the Labour group on the London Assembly, chair of the party's London region and a member of the panel that had interviewed the candidates.

Speaking to the Evening Standard, Duvall stressed the significance of the voting system used for electing the mayor. Under the supplementary vote system, electors can make a first and a second choice of candidate. At the election count, the "first preference" votes are totted up first and unless one candidate has secured more than 50% of the total first preference votes cast, all but the top two candidates are then eliminated. Any "second preference" votes for either of that top two that have cast by electors whose first preference candidate has been knocked out are then added to their respective totals. This "run-off" round of counting produces the final result.

The influence of second preferences on mayoral contests can be over-stated. For example, in 2012 Ken Livingstone's vote total received a bigger second preference boost than Boris Johnson's – 102,355 compared to 82,880. But it was not enough to close the first preference deficit: Johnson had received 971,931 first preferences compared with Livingstone's 889,918. The Conservative therefore won by a final run-off total of 1,054,811 to Livingstone's 992,273, or by 51.53% to 48.47%.

Even so, the boost of roughly 10% that second preferences can give underlined the value to mayoral candidates of being able to appeal to people who might not otherwise vote for the party they represent. Both Johnson and, in his two winning years, Livingstone had been able to do this through the size of their personalities. Duvall was plainly of the view that Jowell, though lacking the celebrity power of either of either "Boris" or "Ken", was the best equipped of the Labour hopefuls to reach beyond party loyalties. "People have got to think carefully about any other candidate in terms of their skills and also how they would attract those second preference votes," he told the Standard.

He also issued a warning: that it would be "extremely damaging" to Labour if, as the Standard paraphrased him, "candidates used group votes to get selected when the process was supposed to be one member, one vote". Duvall was pressed on what that meant by "group votes". Did he have unions in mind? What about mosques? The experienced Duvall gave the measured reply that registered voters should join individually and there should be "no group joining" as that would be an abuse of the system.

If it was a surprise that Duvall had backed Jowell publicly it came as no shock to some that he much preferred her to Khan. Neither was the reference to "group votes" and the Standard's asking Duvall if he had mosques in mind when using that term any mystery to close followers of London politics. In his role as regional chair, Duvall had for years been among those trying to deal with deep-seated Labour troubles in the East End borough of Tower Hamlets, which included the parliamentary seat Oona King had represented until she lost it in a bad tempered 2005 general election battle. There was a long history of splits, factions, feuds and, especially in recent years, allegations of membership irregularities, vote-rigging and Islamist influence from members of the borough's large Bengali community.

In 2010 the borough had elected independent candidate Lutfur Rahman as its first executive mayor after Labour's National Executive Committee had dropped him as Labour candidate following media reports of ties with alleged extremists. Despite more unfriendly coverage and Conservative Communities Secretary Eric Pickles sending financial inspectors into Tower Hamlets Town Hall, Rahman had won again in May 2014, defeating an experienced Labour opponent in local London Assembly member John Biggs. But the following April, Rahman's victory was declared void by a special election court. Grounds for this included that "undue spiritual influence" had been brought to bear on Muslim congregants to support Rahman, with the assistance of a senior local cleric.

On 11 June, Biggs had won the ensuing re-run of the election, from which Rahman was disqualified, taking the number of London boroughs Labour controlled up to 21 out of 32. The result had been a huge relief for Labour, but Duvall's remarks to the Standard were open to the interpretation that he was warning Khan not to copy what Rahman had been found to have done by putting in place any potential faith-based block vote in his favour by organising groups of Muslims, perhaps attached to individual mosques, to sign up as registered Labour supporters. It was certainly how Khan's team interpreted them. Invited to respond, they did so strongly. The Standard carried the following quote:

> "It is deeply offensive to all Londoners that Len Duvall has singled out the Muslim community in his endorsement of Tessa Jowell. We would hope that Tessa distances herself from these comments immediately. You can't become mayor by dividing London and Londoners."

The matter ended there and its beginnings were obscure. Any talk that Khan might be urging "group joining" of the type Duvall warned against did not enjoy a wide circulation. Also, Khan was no ally of Rahman. As co-ordinator of Labour's borough election campaigns in 2014, he had placed Tower Hamlets high on his target list. He and his young political strategist Jack Stenner had attended what turned out to be a marathon and hotly contested count, which took place with a boisterous crowd of Rahman supporters outside the venue. Some in Rahman's camp had been known to disparage Khan, deeming him part and parcel of an Islamophobic Labour establishment.

Whatever the concerns that prompted Duvall's intervention, it ushered the matter of Khan's faith and its potential implications into the mayoral arena for the first time. In one respect it didn't matter how or why that came about. Such was the climate of fearful fascination with Islam among non-Muslims in London as everywhere else, that its arrival had only been a matter of time. The Khan campaign's robust rebuttal of so senior a London Labour figure served notice that anyone it judged to be trying to use Khan's faith against him could expect a strong public rebuke.

The affair, it so happened, took place just after the start of Islam's holy month of Ramadan. Khan, despite the special rigours of the selection race, observed it as usual. Fasting in Britain in the long daylight-hours months of June and July can mean over 16 hours without food or drink. London's variety entailed Khan's maintaining his abstinence in an array of settings, including during a hustings held at a banqueting hall in Southall, a large West London suburb with a predominant South Asian culture - nearly half its population are Hindu, Muslim or, in particular Sikh. Not until the sun had set at the close of the event did he succumb to a buffet of spiced temptations laid out along one wall. Khan is both liberal and devout.

By then, the character of the contest had quietly evolved. Jowell had, to some surprise, accepted a job with a marketing firm that had been closely involved with the Olympics. She had also come under pressure from Lammy, the most abrasive of the six hopefuls, over her liberalization of gambling laws when Culture Secretary and from Abbott over Olympic Park housing. Khan had kept faith with his "winning for a purpose" line, but his portrayal of himself as the "change" candidate and his implied charge that a Mayor Jowell would be little different from Johnson, was understated. Khan's presence on public stages, as on television, was subdued to the point of woodenness. This contrasted curiously with his joshing, livewire off-stage personality. It was, though, no guide to the energy with which his campaign was responding to the suddenly unfolding drama of Labour's national leadership race.

At first, this had been a dull affair. With former ministers Yvette Cooper and Andy Burnham offering little refreshment to an exhausted party's vision, early media interest had focused on Liz Kendall, a younger, newer MP preaching what had become the old time religion of Tony Blair's New Labour. But the party's offer to the British public to help it pick a successor to Ed Miliband was being accepted in such a way that what had seemed wholly implausible in mid-June was starting to look very probable. New members were joining in large numbers. Many other people had become registered supporters, investing in their £3 right to vote. The leadership selectorate was swelling and, most significantly, moving strongly to the left. In late July, the New Statesman's Stephen Bush concluded from a reading of many runes that "Jeremy Corbyn is on course to win the Labour leadership election".

The implications for Labour's mayoral pretenders were clear: London was not being by-passed by this insurgent tide, so the mayoral selectorate was shifting leftwards too. The final non-broadcast hustings was held in Croydon on 10 August, a congenial, mildly de-mob happy affair, to which Jowell sent a stand-in. Croydon is a borough where many of Greater London's larger issues come into focus: population growth and change; high Outer London transport costs for commuters; tensions between high-rise business development and a suburban preservation instinct. Much of the focus was on local concerns.

By contrast, three days later when Khan, Jowell, Abbott and Lammy debated on LBC, the Corbyn surge, as it had become known, was placed centre stage. If it carried the old school left-winger to victory, would Labour face national annihilation? Two or three of those in the studio may have feared so. None said so. Had those who'd nominated

Corbyn for the contest despite not wanting him to be leader been "moronic", as had been suggested? Khan chose his words carefully: it had been right to help Corbyn into the contest, the jury was still out on the electability of all four leadership candidates and: "Whatever you think about Jeremy's policies, he's run a really positive campaign." Would Khan be prepared to serve under Corbyn? A pause: "Probably no." That was as negative as Khan was prepared to be and not, perhaps, without cause.

Voting for mayoral candidate would begin in the next few days. London Labour was saying that 84,000 people had been confirmed as eligible to do so, while a Khan camp source claimed off the record that it was heading fast towards 100,000. There was no question that many of those swelling the ranks were Corbyn supporters. This was not lost on Khan's strategists. His campaign was highly organized. Its number crunchers knew that there was more in "Corbynmania" for them than there could ever be for Jowell. They threw a party for new members. They phone canvassed accordingly. True, Abbott was the natural Corbynite. Wolmar too, Corbyn's fellow Islingtonian, was more of the Corbyn school. But Khan had nominated Corbyn. And Khan, like Corbyn but unlike Jowell, had been critical about Britain's involvement in the Iraq war. Privately, Team Khan predicted that Abbott would finish third ahead of Lammy, but that victory was going to be theirs.

There was another significant development on the day of the LBC debate. A YouGov opinion poll for the station had found that 42% of Londoners thought Jowell the best choice to become next mayor, exactly twice as many as Khan. The poll also found that when offered a straight choice between Jowell and Goldsmith respondents preferred Jowell by 53% to 47%, but when offered the same choice between Khan and Goldsmith, they preferred the Conservative by 54% to 46%. But perhaps the most ominous finding from Khan's point of view concerned attitudes to candidates of his faith. Asked if they would be "comfortable" with a Muslim mayor, 55% of the Londoners asked said yes, but a large minority of 31% said the opposite.

LBC at first misreported this result on its website, claiming the poll had shown that half of Londoners would be uncomfortable with a Muslim mayor rather than less than a third of them. Marcus Roberts, Khan's selection campaign manager, wrote a strongly-worded letter of complaint. This addressed not only the misreporting of the figures, but the focus on the issue in the first place:

> *"People are perhaps inevitably anxious about faiths they don't know and that is why Sadiq has spent so much of his adult life reaching out across communities to increase understanding. I hope you can reassure me – and Londoners – that your*

coverage of these issues does not run the risk of undermining the strength of our city with questions that fuel prejudice and risk setting Londoners against each other."

The responsibilities of London mayors primarily involve transport, housing, planning, policing and economic growth. Whatever the rights and wrongs of the YouGov "Muslim mayor" question and whatever the relevance of his attitudes to Corbyn, it was already clear that Sadiq Khan and those around him were primed and ready for political opponents to try to make his battle to win City Hall about something other than what he'd actually do if he got there.

*****

As Labour's aspiring mayors strained as hard for every small advantage they decently could, their Conservative counterparts went about their business with, by comparison, immense tranquility. There were four in the Tory field, chosen after interviews with members of their party's London region leadership. All of them were male following the perhaps surprising exclusion of Westminster City Council leader Philippa Roe. It was, however, still an eclectic group, demonstrating that the party of queen, country and green, pleasant Englishness could accommodate London's vaunted human diversity too.

Andrew Boff, who at the time headed the Conservative group on the London Assembly, had been the leader of suburban Hillingdon Council before moving to the Labour stronghold of Hackney where he made his presence felt as a councillor and activist despite being severely outnumbered. Gay, a cyclist and firmly on his party's libertarian wing, Boff's bid to become the Tory mayoral candidate included the idea of binding much of the south-east of England more closely to London in a Thames City "southern powerhouse" and trialing a managed street prostitution area with a view to better protecting vulnerable sex workers and enabling their trade to be policed more effectively.

The Tory quartet also contained Syed Kamall, one of London's European Parliament members. Kamall is a Muslim son of immigrants, whose father was a London bus driver – the symmetry with Khan could hardly have been more exquisite. A member of Boris Johnson's administration was trying his luck, too. Since 2012, Stephen Greenhalgh had headed the Mayor's Office for Policing and Crime. In that capacity he had purchased four second hand water cannon which the Home Secretary then banned the use of and busied himself filling a large funding gap by selling off land owned by the Metropolitan Police with the relish of a born privatizer. Before that, Greenhalgh had led a radical

Hammersmith and Fulham Council administration which was said to have been David Cameron's favourite local authority.

All three had distinctive strengths. All were doomed to trail the Richmond dreamboat. Perhaps belying his laid back manner, Goldsmith enjoys gambling. In 2004 he won £53,000 in a televised card game. In 2005 he took part in the first World Spoofing Championship, a pub betting game to decide who buys the next round of drinks. Various Goldsmiths, Rothschilds and Astors took part under the auspices of Ladbrokes. Many £50 notes were flourished. Goldsmith won. The Conservative has a stake in the elite Mayfair bookmaker Fitzdares. If they'd offered odds on his chances of becoming the Tory candidate, they would have been extremely short.

The first public hustings of the Tory selection race was held amid the plush of the Institute of Directors headquarters in Pall Mall. "I believe London has been incredibly well served over the last eight years by Boris Johnson," Goldsmith told a full house. It was thanks to Johnson, he declared, that none could now doubt that the British capital was the greatest city in the world. Even, so, it faced challenges: rapid population growth meant enormous pressure on the transport system, the "living environment" and, perhaps most of all, on housing. This demanded a mayor who could "secure a good deal from government" but was also "willing and able to hold government to account when it gets it wrong".

These were trailers for the coming conflict with whomever Goldsmith would face from Labour: basking in the "Boris" glory; boasting of a bond with fellow Tories in national government that would be co-operative but not subservient. On housing, Goldsmith said that the answer to high house prices and rents was to increase supply and that the key to this lay in publically-owned land. Transport for London had a vast portfolio, which they were already starting to develop. London's boroughs owned vast acreages.

Goldsmith elaborated. "Some local authorities own more than a third of the land within their borders," he revealed. In short, there was a wealth of London territory that could be "released for development". Once liberated, this trapped ground would be the seedbed for "homes that Londoners actually want". By this, Goldsmith meant "high density, low-rise buildings which are in keeping with communities". This would not simply be so that development would be "beautiful" but also so as not to "exhaust the appetite Londoners have for the development we need". Here was a hallmark Goldsmith principle: "If we react *en masse* against development, it's going to be much harder to deliver the quantity of homes that we need."

The audience raised two awkward questions. One concerned the green belt. Comprising 22% of the 600 square miles enclosed by Greater London, this land has been protected against development for 60 years with very few incursions. Would it be safe under a Mayor Goldsmith? "I don't think we need to even consider developing the green belt for now," Goldsmith said and drew a "red line" around it. He did, though, allow a caveat to this: "It may be that the population explodes and 15 or 20 years down the line we'll have to have the discussion again." For now, though, he would concentrate elsewhere. Those "brownfield" borough holdings were at the top of his list along with the housing built on them: "Badly-designed 1950s, 1960s estates which could be redeveloped at higher density and to a better quality."

The second awkward question concerned the reluctance of some boroughs to encourage much house building. Former minister David Willetts, the Tory policy brain who chaired the hustings, likened these to EU countries reluctant to take in refugees (although he didn't mention Britain by name). Boroughs answering that description tend to be Tory-run. Goldsmith the localist spoke up for borough autonomy, saying it would be "a mistake for the mayor to flex his muscles without taking into account the legitimate views of local authorities". But: "I think the mayor has sufficient power to prompt those boroughs that are sleepy. Ultimately, every borough's going to have to play a role if we are going to avoid this crisis."

A woman inquired about tall buildings, whose proliferation under Johnson had spawned a Save Our Skyline campaign. She cited skyscrapers going up beside the Thames in Vauxhall and the north of Battersea as part of the massive Nine Elms development, describing these in a distressed tone as "hideous beyond speech". She voiced distaste that they were being sold "off plan" – that is, on the strength of marketing images before even being built – in Malaysia and bought by "very, very wealthy people". She asked: "Where are ordinary people supposed to live?"

Goldsmith expressed sympathy. "A lot of the buildings that are going up are being bought by people effectively as safe deposit boxes that no-one is going to live in," he agreed, although he cautioned that it was unclear quite how many really were being left vacant. However, he felt sure that the eagerness of the world's super rich to sink mountains of loose cash into future London bricks and mortar could be used to London's advantage: "I would suggest that we turn that into a good, not a bad" - indeed an "overwhelming positive". Goldsmith said he would "ensure that that money was geared to building homes for Londoners. Not the blocks that you've just described, but homes that people can live in". Goldsmith felt sure that this was possible. There would also be "fundamentally, a London first bias in relation to the homes that are being built and bought".

The hustings provided a good summary of Goldsmith's stance on housing. Going against the populist mood against foreign investment, he welcomed this manifestation of freely moving global capital. For him, it provided one of the three essentials for speeding up house building: planning powers, finance and land. He stressed that the other two were also available: the mayor's planning powers were considerable and the public sector possessed that untapped wealth of land. Brought together, this trinity was potentially transformative, though he made clear that in practice it would be regulated by aesthetic and democratic values dear to his heart. There would be no roughshod riding over local feeling. And a particular concept of beauty would guide the Goldsmith way.

*****

The four Tories met again on the radio a few days later. Answering a question from an LBC listener, Goldsmith filled in another piece of his provisional housing policy picture. He identified housing costs as "the central question" for addressing the city's high cost of living. This was the main thing that was "pricing Londoners out of London". He had a particular category of Londoner most in mind: "I think there is a really important gap in the market that needs to be filled, and that's for people aged between, say, 25 and 40 and earning around £25-40,000; people who, at the moment, are spending more than half their income on rent." Goldsmith pointed out that such households were not eligible for social housing, but neither could they save the deposit they needed to get a mortgage on a home of their own. Goldsmith said there was "a huge, crying need to provide houses for those people".

As the show went on, a fuller portrait of some of Goldsmith's driving passions emerged. Boff, who would later be hailed the star of the Tory contest by the influential website Conservative Home, challenged him over his attitude to a planned new bridge across the Thames in Central London that Boris Johnson was championing. The proposed Garden Bridge had become controversial for several reasons, not least the suspicion that Johnson's backing for it owed something to his long-standing family friendship with the veteran comic actress Joanna Lumley, who had known Johnson since he was a small child.

Lumley had come up with the Garden Bridge idea and been lobbying for it for many years, painting word pictures of a pedestrian walkway cascading with flora in her hallmark breathy tones. In an interview, she had described "dear Boris" as "largely quite amenable". Johnson had required a reluctant Transport for London to invest £30m in the project. Goldsmith was keen on it. Boff, a sceptic, asked him what he might have spent the £30m on instead. Useful things, perhaps, like a bunch of cleaner buses or some new rail infrastructure? Goldsmith acknowledged concerns among some local people and about the rising cost of the project. But even so: "I know I'm in a minority on this panel, but I think it's an attractive design. It caught my imagination when I first saw it. It's the kind of project that I think future generations will look at with fondness."

There followed a discussion about traffic congestion. A caller from Brixton suggested the congestion charge should be increased to help improve air quality and help businesses. For many Tories, the charge had always been just another tax on private motorists and an intrusion on individual freedom. Boff had never been keen. He thought the levy inefficient to collect and soon to be made redundant by Johnson's forthcoming ultra low emission zone – the ULEZ, for short - which would cover the same area and impose a charge on the owners of polluting vehicles entering it. Boff wasn't sold on that either. He would have preferred a fining system, because: "What we're aiming for is clean air, not to allow rich people to pollute."

Goldsmith took a different line. He thought the congestion charge system "clunky and old-fashioned" but was sure congestion would be worse without it. He agreed with Boff that the ULEZ would surpass it, but said there was a case for being "more bullish, more ambitious than the current plan. So, a bigger area…"

Presenter Iain Dale cut in. "How far would you expand the congestion charge?" he asked. Goldsmith said it was too early to answer that. Dale pressed: "Push it out to Kensington, as before?" Livingstone had extended the charging zone westwards. Johnson, whilst retaining the original Central London charging zone, had scrapped the extension. Was Goldsmith planning to bring it back again?

"I don't know where it would go," Goldsmith replied, saying he would defer to local boroughs. He was, though, sure there was "a case to be made for expanding it and ramping up the fines for people who fail to meet the standards".

A degree of ambiguity had entered the proceedings by this stage. Dale had asked about expanding congestion charging. Goldsmith seemed to be talking about a larger ULEZ than the one Johnson had approved but, if so, he hadn't corrected Dale. Congestion charging was such an emotive political issue that even Livingstone had decided against pledging to restore the western extension when running against Johnson in 2012. Hence Dale's eager interest. The Evening Standard had the same impression about what Goldsmith had meant. "Tory Zac Goldsmith has said he could expand the congestion charge if he is elected Mayor of London," went its topline.

Soon after, Goldsmith issued a clarification. No, he didn't favour more congestion charging. And, by the way, the current system was outdated. Dale had observed that many Tories and Tory voters had fought tooth and nail against the congestion charge. Goldsmith had said he thought those days were gone. It seemed that others had advised him otherwise.

*****

The Royal Festival Hall in the Southbank arts complex was the glamorous, Thames-side venue for Labour's announcement of its candidate. The date was 11 September. The previous day, the Evening Standard had announced its "unambiguous" view that Tessa Jowell would be the best choice for Labour. This was surprising only for its timing, which was too late to influence voters. "It might be taken that the Standard thinks it is backing a winner," observed the Labour List website. Certainly, Jowell's team had been asserting its belief that it would win.

As the candidates emerged into the spotlight from a side room, the two frontrunners spoke very different body languages. Jowell smiled at supporters in the audience. Khan's expression was a study in unreadability.

Len Duvall read out the results for each section of the selectorate round-by-round, with impeccable neutrality. The single transferable vote electoral system used meant candidates were eliminated one by one. Thomas was the first to be knocked out. Khan led. He remained in the lead after the second round, which saw Wolmar excluded, and the third, when Lammy was eliminated. By then it was clear that he would win. Abbott was the next to be removed, finishing third as Khan's team had predicted. That left Khan and Jowell. The split between the two in the final round was Khan 58.9%, Jowell 41.1%. Khan was the very clear winner.

Some reports called it a shock win, but the only true surprise was the scale of it: 48,152 votes to 33,573. Afterwards, Khan declared his pleasure in having finished top in all three categories of voter: affiliated members, the £3 registered supporters and full party members. He'd only overtaken Jowell among the latter group in the final round, however, finishing with 24,983 votes to her 24,019. Among affiliates, he took 5,990 votes to Jowell's 3,203. But it was the £3 registered supporters who helped him most of all against Jowell: by 17,179 to 6,351.

In his speech, Khan said he was "deeply humbled" by the support he had received and pledged to provide "more opportunities for all Londoners". He set out his priorities for them: "An affordable and secure home to rent or buy, more jobs with higher wages for the lowest paid, making it easier to set up and run a successful business, reducing the cost of commuting, and making London's environment safer, healthier and less polluted."

Afterwards, he huddled with journalists. Martin Hoscik, who writes the respected MayorWatch website, put it to him that he would find it hard to work with Labour borough leaders who had supported Jowell. As he spoke, Lib Peck, the leader of Lambeth Council who had lined up behind the former Olympics minister, was coming down an adjacent set of stairs. Khan called out to her: "Hey, Lib, we'll be able to work together, won't me?"

"No problem," Peck replied.

"There you go," said Khan, turning to Hoscik once more: "That's how it's done."

To the Guardian, he disclosed his feelings about the contest as it had progressed. "I never thought it was going to be a close race," he said: "I was always quietly confident."

*****

The Conservative candidate was announced three weeks later, on 2 October. There was far less ceremony than with Labour. Indeed, there was no ceremony at all. No event. No gathering. No live countdown to the final score. Instead, a press release was dispatched. It said that Goldsmith had won, securing 6,514 votes out of the 9,227 cast. Syed Kamall came second with 1,477 votes,

Stephen Greenhalgh third with 864 and Andrew Boff fourth with 372. It was a stroll for Goldsmith, as expected.

More revealing was the turnout and what it said about the respective grassroots strengths of the two main parties in the capital. Unlike Labour, the Tories had conducted a fully open primary. As well as London party members, any London resident could take part in the ballot if they signed up for just £1. Yet there had been no mass participation. Instead had come reports of technical problems depriving some who wished to register of the chance to vote. From the camp of one candidate came grumbles that the whole process had looked "chaotic" compared with Labour's and that too little effort had been put into marketing it. Whatever was to blame, nearly ten times as many people – 87,884 – voted in the Labour process than the Tory one. The "tens of thousands" Khan had thanked for helping him prevail alone far outnumbered all those who had taken part in the Tory selection ballot put together.

For this reason as well as recent electoral history, Goldsmith depicted himself as the underdog. He also moved again to hitch his wagon to Mayor Johnson, saying he'd want to build on his legacy: "Anyone who tried to put themselves in Boris's shoes would be mad. Boris is unique in British politics. He's mobbed in the streets by people from left and right. He spends half his time doing selfies. That's not the kind of mayoralty we will have after May, whoever wins the election. But Boris is a very serious figure. His record stands up to serious scrutiny. There's been huge progress for seven years. My job is to not put that at risk, and to build on it."

Three

Positioning

It would be hard to overstate the speed and eagerness with which Sadiq Khan moved to express disapproval of everything about Jeremy Corbyn that posed a threat to his hopes of becoming mayor. Just five days after Corbyn was crowned Labour leader, an interview with Khan appeared in the Financial Times, daily journal of the capitalist class.

The new Labour leader had appointed as his shadow chancellor John McDonnell, MP for the West London constituency of Hayes and Harlington and another veteran of his party's leftmost wing. McDonnell was an advocate of nationalizing banks and imposing big tax hikes on high earners and City profits. His Who's Who entry declared a cheery zest for overthrowing capitalism.

Khan offered a very different view. He said that, unlike McDonnell, he didn't want more taxes on businesses and was eager to attract more businesses to London. "If business does well, London does well," he said and placed on record what would become a signature campaign pledge to become "the most business-friendly mayor of all time."

Two days after that, Corbyn himself was criticised by Khan in the pages of the stridently nationalistic Mail on Sunday. The previous week, in one of his first public duties in his new role, Corbyn had failed to sing the national anthem during a ceremony to mark the 75th anniversary of the Battle of Britain. This, according to Khan, had been "very unwise and disrespectful".

There had been speculation that Corbyn would refuse to participate in the arcane process for inducting him into the Queen's advisory Privy Council, which involves senior politicians kneeling before the monarch, swearing a loyalty oath and bestowing upon her a *faux* kiss in the form of letting their nose brush the back of her outstretched hand.

Khan recalled doing all this on becoming a member of Gordon Brown's cabinet as transport minister, but holding a Koran rather than a Bible. He described being teased for the enthusiasm with which he'd undergone this ritual abasement and harked back to a patriotic childhood. He even provided the newspaper with a childhood photograph of himself and some of his siblings at a Silver Jubilee street party in 1977. "My family's always been proud of being British," he declared.

Wading into darker waters, Khan rebuked Corbyn for his sympathies with Middle East armed groups in conflict with Israel, saying these fortified "the perception at the last election that Labour is anti-Jewish". He added: "Whenever there is tension in the Middle East it leads to anti-Semitism in our country. There are Jewish schools and synagogues in London, which need round-the-clock security. I will have a zero-tolerance of anti-Semitism – it's not acceptable in 21st Century London."

In saying these things for the benefit of Mail on Sunday readers, Khan would have been particularly mindful of two things. One was the acrimonious collapse that had taken place in the relationship between Jewish Londoners and Ken Livingstone. These had largely arisen from Livingstone's history of criticisms of Israel but had been given an added, domestic, impetus in 2005 after Livingstone, departing a party to mark the 20th anniversary of the first MP to come out as gay, had acerbically put it to an Evening Standard reporter that he was "just like a concentration camp guard, you are just doing it because you are paid to, aren't you?" The reporter was Jewish. A resulting four-week suspension imposed on Livingstone was later quashed by a judge, but the stain on his reputation in some eyes was indelible.

The second, partly related, factor that would have been in Khan's mind was Labour's failure in May to win parliamentary seats in the North London borough of Barnet, which has a large Jewish population, despite the party's making gains in the capital as a whole. The Hendon constituency was a knife-edge marginal which Labour had seemed certain to regain having lost it in 2010 by just 106 votes. Instead, the Tory majority increased. Finchley and Golders Green was a much tougher target but the combination of a strong Jewish candidate and an encouraging local opinion poll had given Labour hope. In the end, the Tories held it easily.

The Mail on Sunday termed Khan's remarks "a devastating assault" on Corbyn's leadership. They and his comments to the Financial Times marked the start of a sustained construction of defences by Khan against predictable and potentially damaging lines of attack. Defining himself as independent of Corbyn would have been a key requirement for Khan under any circumstances. The fact of having helped him into Labour's leadership contest made the conspicuous digging of a wide trench between them a more urgent matter still.

Although there had not been time to pick through the wreckage of Ed Miliband's general election defeat, it was plain that he and Labour had been seen by electors as ill-equipped to run the British economy in line with their idea of competence. At first sight, therefore, the significantly more left-wing Corbyn-McDonnell combination could hardly have been better designed to erode voter confidence in Labour still more. Corbyn's ship looked destined for the seabed almost as soon as it was launched. Khan had no intention of being dragged under by it.

Khan's comments about patriotism, terrorism and Jews were another demonstration of his wish to place himself at barge-pole distance from his new party leader. They also betrayed an acute awareness of his need to pass what might be called the Muslim Test – a very public examination of his adherence to benchmark tenets of Britishness and liberal social values. This test, intangible yet exacting, was being set for British Muslims in general by many in the media and in every day life by much of the public as part of a national and global climate where the loyalty of Muslims to the Western societies in which many millions live was being endlessly inspected and doubted.

It was essential for Khan to pass the Muslim Test. Even in intensely multicultural London, overt anti-Muslim sentiment and, perhaps even more corrosively, nagging suspicions about covert, sinister Muslim attitudes and sympathies were a danger to Khan's campaign. His remarks to the Mail on Sunday were a bold and ruthless move to insulate himself against such sentiments among non-Muslims and pre-empt any attempt by enemies to mobilise them.

Defending Jews was integral to this. Labour's national stance on Palestine had hurt it among Jewish Londoners, notwithstanding the heritage of Miliband, the son of the eminent Jewish academic

Ralph Miliband who'd fled to Britain as a child to escape Nazi persecution. As a Muslim, it was imperative for Khan to uncouple himself from that Labour legacy. He travelled to a café in East Finchley to tell the Jewish Chronicle that if he became mayor he would want "zero tolerance of anti-Semitism". Over the summer he'd begun his Ramadan fast at synagogues, seeking ways to increase inter-faith overlap. Jews and Muslims, he said, had "a huge amount" in common.

There were other groups of Londoners Khan also wished to reassure. Recent figures had shown a rise in recorded hate crimes in the capital. Political reporter Rachel Holdsworth of the website Londonist invited Khan to respond to them. "I would make it quite clear [as mayor and in charge of policing] that there would be zero tolerance of anti-Semitism, Islamophobia and homophobia," he said.

The last of these was picked up approvingly by the website Pink News. For hardline Islamists, like Christian fundamentalists, homosexuality is an abomination. Khan had no intention of being tainted by such associations. He told Holdsworth: "Too often the people who are 'representing' the Islamic faith aren't representative, they're angry men with beards. And that is not what Islam is about." If he failed the Muslim Test, it would not be for want of trying.

*****

Fresh from their respective triumphs, both Khan and Goldsmith addressed the annual conferences of their respective parties. Labour's came first, at the end of September in Brighton. Khan's speech was unexceptional but functional. It opened with a joke about Brighton being known in Tooting as "London-by-the-Sea." This was not, perhaps, as sociologically acute as the bohemian seaside city's better-known nickname of "Hackney-on-Sea" but it enabled Khan to again underline his proletarian pedigree by reminiscing about workers' family outings to the south coast on board a double decker; about "ice cream, the pier and fish and chips – the proper seaside experience". Proper London. Proper Brit.

Khan said his one reason for seeking the mayoralty was to extend to others the opportunities he'd enjoyed when he was younger. Again, he paid tribute to support from institutions of the state. But he also again pledged to be "the most pro-business mayor ever, helping create jobs and wealth" as well as promising to make transport costs affordable and to fight for the London Living Wage, a voluntary rate set higher than the mandatory national minimum wage in order to reflect the capital's higher living costs. He added that he would defend British membership of the

European Union. David Cameron, prompted by concerns that Tory voters were drifting towards the anti-EU United Kingdom Independence Party, had promised to hold a referendum on remaining in the EU later in the year. Khan was keen to draw a contrast between himself and Goldsmith, a long-standing Eurosceptic like his late father.

His biggest line, though, was on housing: "I'm going to make the election in May a referendum on London's housing crisis." He told his audience about sleeping on the bunk bed at his parents' house until he was in his mid-twenties and how this helped him and his wife buy their first home. He challenged Goldsmith to join him in opposing the government's controversial Housing and Planning Bill. It was an offer Khan knew the Conservative could only refuse. Significantly, as well as speaking up for his council house background, Khan said he aimed to "make Labour the party of home ownership".

The following week, Goldsmith addressed the Conservative conference in Manchester. He too majored on housing, saying there had been "a giant shift" in public attitudes in his constituency since he'd been selected to contest it in 2008. Back then, he said, "Candidates were asked, 'who will fight off the developers?'" But now their question was different. It was: "How the hell are our kids going to get homes to live in?" He added: "Londoners are being priced out of their own city."

Goldsmith offered an answer to these problems. It was, he said, "Not easy. But it is simple. We need to build". He reprised his argument about there being plenty of land to build on without "destroying the green spaces we love" and said that "put together, Transport for London land alone would be bigger than the borough of Camden". He again stressed that there was no shortage of the finance required for building homes. Though accepting that properties purchased and left empty caused resentment Goldsmith argued, as he had at the Prospect and Centre for London hustings, that it was good that what he called "outside investors" saw London as "a safe bet".

Goldsmith developed his case that this situation presented a choice: "We can close the door to outside investors, which is what the Labour Party wants to do. Or we can capture that finance and use it to build the homes we need on publicly owned land." A Mayor Goldsmith, he said, would "set up a fund designed specifically to attract big institutional investors," and use that fund for the building of "a new generation" of "affordable homes for young people who neither qualify for housing lists nor are able to buy, but who have to spend most of their income on rent".

Goldsmith re-stated his "important caveat" that development should respect local communities and not be "dumped on them" against their wishes, but insisted that "if we work with communities and give them a real say, then the opportunities are endless". Where might such opportunities be located? "Consider the 3,500 1950s and 60s estates, many of them poorly designed, many of them coming to the end of their lives," Goldsmith said: "With the consent of the local community – and with guarantees that they won't be fragmented – we have a chance to rebuild them and provide more homes, better communities and more beautiful streetscapes." He added: "If I am elected mayor, I will ensure that local communities can vote to require the mayor to call in significant developments." Such voting rights, he said, would "make direct democracy in London reality".

The two candidates' words about housing to their respective parties' conferences provided an outline of important differences and some similarities between them. Khan stressed the social value of council housing but included in that value the scope a social rent could create for saving for a deposit and moving out of social housing and into home ownership, as his parents had.

To a degree this aligned him with arguments made by London Conservatives, notably Stephen Greenhalgh, that social housing should be a launch pad to something better rather than a lifetime destination. In this, there was a recognition by Khan that home ownership remains a huge aspiration for many renting Londoners, perhaps more so rather than less as a result of its becoming ever harder for them to meet. While pledging allegiance to his party's historic defence of council housing, Khan was also signaling empathy with despairing would-be first-time buyers – a growing section of the London demographic.

But Goldsmith's housing pitch was the more revealing. Some of his language and statistics were familiar. That is because another politician had used them a few months earlier. Writing in the June edition of Prospect, Andrew Adonis, a Labour peer who had once led Tony Blair's policy unit and had backed Tessa Jowell's mayoral bid, had described how he would address the housing crisis, especially in London.

His article had begun by making a distinction between the words "simple" and "easy". Adonis wrote that his experience in government had taught him that effective solutions to large problems could be uncomplicated in theory yet difficult politically because of the opposition they could meet. Goldsmith's speech precisely echoed these linguistic definitions: the answer to the problem of building more homes would be "not easy" but it was "simple".

Adonis's article had gone on to identify the best sort of land for urban development as being mostly owned by public sector authorities, notably in the capital. He'd singled out Transport for London as one of the largest public landowners, just as Goldsmith did in his conference speech. He'd also mentioned "an estimated 3,500 large council estates" in London, the same figure Goldsmith used.

The Labour thinker's views on what should be done with those estates also echoed in Goldsmith's conference address. "The regeneration of existing council estates is a vitally important element" he'd written, citing a London Assembly housing committee report which had found that only about 50 had been substantially redeveloped since their construction in times when London's housing needs had been very different. In line with a collection of essays he had edited for the left-of-centre Institute for Public Policy Research think tank, published in March, Adonis proposed the demolition of these estates and their replacement with what he called "city villages" – mixed tenure developments with higher densities, also containing community facilities and business premises, that were better designed than what they had replaced.

The close similarities between what Goldsmith told the Tory faithful in Manchester in early October and what Adonis had advocated a few months earlier were entertaining and also raised suspicions. The day before Goldsmith spoke in Manchester, the Guardian reported that Adonis would be resigning the Labour whip in the House of Lords after being signed up by Chancellor George Osborne to head a new National Infrastructure

Commission. Osborne's own conference speech confirmed this news.

The move's meaning in the context of Corbyn's leadership triumph was unmistakable. The Guardian quoted a Tory source: "I think you can see what Andrew Adonis thinks of Labour's prospects." Adonis let it be known that, despite the striking resemblances between his Prospect article and Goldsmith's speech, he had not been assisting the Tory mayoral runner with his housing policy – and, after all, even if Goldsmith or his researchers had read his Prospect piece, which seemed distinctly possible, that was not evidence of collusion. The real significance of the close likeness was that it demonstrated the extent to which Labour and Conservative policy blueprints for estates could overlap in a London setting, as indeed they already did on the ground. In some Labour-run boroughs, major estate regeneration schemes had been completed or were underway.

The core principles were identical. The differences between Adonis's proposals and Goldsmith's lay only in the details they set out. The potential significance of these varied. Goldsmith's pledge to give communities the right to vote on whether a development scheme should be "called in" by the mayor was novel. It did not, though, amount to giving those communities a veto over plans they did not like, only a right to secure a mandate binding a potential future Mayor

Goldsmith to consider exercising his own veto, either by using his considerable planning powers to tell the borough concerned to reconsider the plans or by appropriating the determination of the scheme himself. So far as could be gleaned from Goldsmith's speech, such a "direct democracy" vote by communities would place the mayor under no obligation to exercise those powers, merely to consider doing so.

Goldsmith's speech also left open the large question of how he would define the communities concerned. Adonis's Prospect article referred directly and exclusively to the "hundreds or thousands of families" for whom estates are home and stressed that "gaining their participation and consent to change is essential". But Goldsmith's notional communities deserving of empowerment were less precisely described in his speech. In praising individual estate regenerations, Adonis mentioned the social housing component of their mix of tenure types and had previously insisted that the creation of his "city villages" would entail no net loss of such units.

When talking about estates, Goldsmith mentioned "guarantees" that the "local community" would not "be fragmented". However, he did not mention social housing in his speech at all, only new homes for private purchase affordable to people who would never qualify for it. What were his plans for Londoners for whom social renting is the only affordable option?

*****

On 9 October, three days after Goldsmith's conference speech, the first poll of the campaign proper was published. Conducted by YouGov, which had a good record for measuring Londoners' voting intentions in past mayoral elections, it showed Khan and Goldsmith running just about neck-and-neck with a large portion of those surveyed undecided.

The "not sure" group accounted for 44%. Of the rest, 29% preferred Khan and 28% Goldsmith. The sample Londoners were also asked their views on how the two men would cope in a crisis, whether they were "likeable" and whether they were in touch with ordinary people. In each of these three categories there were again more than 40% who were unsure, rising to 55% for the "crisis" question. In two of them, the outcome was again extremely close. The exception was the "in touch" response. Here, Khan was well ahead by 41% to 18%. In this respect, the bus driver's son looked streets ahead.

In early November, Khan made his first public appearance with Jeremy Corbyn since their respective ballot-topping performances. They joined forces outside Arsenal Football Club,

Corbyn's local team, to support a campaign to get the capital's Premier League clubs to pay all its employees the London Living Wage. Such occasions would remain rare.

Then, the Muslim Test was set again and not by a pollster. On the night of 13 November in Paris, gunmen and suicide bombers of the fundamentalist group known as Islamic State of Iraq and the Levant – ISIL, ISIS, IS or sometimes Daesh for short - attacked restaurants and bars, a concert hall and the Stade de France sports stadium, killing 130 people. Three days later, the British government gave orders that its security forces should take a "shoot to kill" approach to perpetrators of similar atrocities in the UK. Corbyn voiced reservations about this before saying that as Prime Minister he would permit "proportionate" use of the measure in order to protect life. But in the Commons on 17 November Cameron accused him of ambiguity on the issue.

Two days later, Khan addressed parliament's political journalists. It is not unusual for Westminster politicians to speak to gatherings of parliamentary reporters, but this was a high stakes occasion for Khan. It was already no secret that Goldsmith's campaign and Conservative-supporting newspapers were sniffing around for ways to depict him as an apologist for, or even a sympathiser with, Muslim extremists. In the wake of Paris one perceived equivocation, one word that could be presented as being out of place, would have been seized on by Khan's enemies and used to punish him until polling day.

Judging by the coverage his words received, Khan's decision to speak to the political journalists was a good one. He emerged from the occasion undamaged and fortified. His words contained some barely-coded criticisms of Corbyn's handling of royal protocol and attitude to national security. An appeal to his fellow British Muslims to embrace a "special role" they could play in combatting extremism in their own country was prominently reported by the Evening Standard. The Daily Telegraph, which, with its Sunday counterpart, is a habitual source of tales of homegrown Islamist conspiracies, reported his words neutrally and soberly.

The Daily Mail, a paper fond of stories about one dire threat or other to the British way of life, picked up on his observation that "too many British Muslims grow up without really knowing anyone from a different background" and his claim that the political establishment has, for too long, "tolerated segregation" at the expense of "creating a common life". More out of character, the Mail also quoted Khan's remark that: "Too many British people have never befriended a Muslim." And his expression of paternal concern that his teenage daughters "could be groomed by extremists on the internet" was also picked up by Britain's most stridently "pro-family" news title.

Khan's words were carefully crafted to please his potentially dangerous audience and, as such, to place some very important bricks in his defensive wall. So anxious were those words to please that some might have damned them as tipping over into appeasement. Yet the line Khan took, which sought to condemn extremism in the plainest terms and urge his fellow Muslims to take a lead in fighting it without denying the hostility they faced from some of their fellow citizens, was consistent with arguments he'd made before, notably in his Fabian Society pamphlet in 2008.

This pedigree lent Khan's speech an authenticity it might otherwise have been suspected of lacking. So did the passage in which he described being "subjected to a campaign of hate" each time he'd run for parliament on the grounds that he was placing democracy above religious law. Being able to tell of such experiences had the benefit of emphasizing what promised to be a source of strength in the campaign – street level experiences that many fellow Londoners could relate to and Goldsmith had never known.

But Islamist violence and how best to combat it was soon to present Khan with another delicate parliamentary challenge. A week later, the Prime Minister set out his case for extending bombing raids by British aircraft against IS fighters from Iraq across the border into Syria. A Commons debate and vote were held on 2 December, with Labour severely split. Corbyn opposed the action but his shadow foreign secretary Hilary Benn made a powerful speech in favour. A further 65 Labour MPs joined Benn in helping Cameron secure a comfortable majority, including 11 from London. Khan, though, was one of 29 London MPs who voted against. The others included his three fellow London Muslim MPs, Tulip Siddiq, Rupa Huq and Rushanara Ali. Currently: Khan had hinted at his intentions earlier, saying his top priority was "keeping Londoners safe". Goldsmith backed extending the bombing.

The following day, a second YouGov poll since the candidates were chosen gave Khan a six-point lead over Goldsmith among respondents likely to vote – a five-point increase compared with October. The survey was conducted between 18 and 21 November, well before the Syria bombing debate. However, its outcome could have been affected by Khan's words to the men and women of the press gallery, which had been so widely and positively reported.

The detail of the poll gave good reasons, were they required, for guarding against over-confidence. As well as showing that Khan was more popular than Goldsmith among women voters – a knock back for any assumption that London's females would melt into the Tory's arms – they found that while the Labour man was also strongly favoured by the young, Goldsmith was well ahead among older voters, who tend to be more likely to vote. Even so, the poll could hardly be interpreted as bad news for Khan, not least because it gave grounds for hope that the Muslim Test might be passed.

*****

London life was not very noticeably disrupted as a result the Paris attacks. As Christmas approached, shoppers thronged and commuters squeezed on to public transport as before. London Underground reported carrying record numbers of passengers. There was, though, an undercurrent of unease: people of measured judgment confessed to steering clear of the most crowded places and eschewing the Tube when possible; the Met recorded a rise in anti-Muslim hate crimes; on 5 December at Leytonstone station on the Central Line a man with a knife assailed passengers, inflicting serious neck injuries on one of them. Witnesses reported him shout: "This is for Syria."

Against this backdrop, on 7 December, the Goldsmith campaign unveiled its strategy for defeating Khan. An official Conservative website called SadiqWatch asked the question: "Who is Sadiq Khan?" It drew attention to Khan's recent change of position over Heathrow, the support he'd received from unions, the backing he'd received from Ken Livingstone and his nomination of Corbyn. Goldsmith had previously said it would be wise of him to listen to the advice of Lynton Crosby, the Australian election strategist who had steered Boris Johnson to his two mayoral election wins and Cameron to his general election majority. Goldsmith had since hired the services of Crosby's company and appointed his senior colleague Mark Fullbrook as his campaign director.

Crosby's successes in Britain and elsewhere had owed much to the clever cultivation of voter anxiety, using insinuation about emotive issues to mobilize support. SadiqWatch was a regulation example of this negative campaigning style. The site brought more fully into the public arena the Goldsmith campaign's attempts to detrimentally associate Khan with Corbyn. Its masthead proclaimed that it was "holding Corbyn's candidate to account". It made much of Khan's nominating Corbyn to enter the Labour leadership race, but didn't mention that he hadn't voted for Corbyn in the ballot.

Goldsmith campaign material literature being distributed by activists described Khan's politics as "radical and divisive". These words prompted an immediate response from Khan's team. One of its members told the Evening Standard they could be read as "code for Muslim" and a "coded racist attack" – a "dog whistle" to anti-Muslim sentiment.

Goldsmith's campaign responded in turn, saying it was "utterly predictable that Labour label their opponents as racists". They cited Livingstone doing the same thing to Johnson during their mayoral battles and concluded: "Now Ken and Corbyn's cronies are doing it again." Defending the use of the term "radical" to denigrate Khan, they produced three past examples of it being applied to him favourably.

One was an article from January for a website called Left Futures written by veteran activist Jon Lansman, who had been organizing grassroots support for Corbyn. Lansman had argued in his piece that Khan was misusing his position as shadow minister for London to advance a covert mayoral candidacy bid. It had, however, opened by described Khan approvingly as a "former radical human rights lawyer". Another example given was a headline that had appeared in April on Khan's Tooting general election website above a link to an article in The Voice newspaper about the launch of Labour's general election manifesto for black and other ethnic minority voters. It read: "Labour's radical plans to tackle race inequality." The third was a New Statesman piece from August by Hammersmith MP Andy Slaughter in which he had described Khan's mayoral agenda as "radical and bold".

As justifications for the Goldsmith campaign's attempts to cast Khan in a perturbing light, these were unpersuasive. There is nothing inherently negative about politicians of any stripe being called radical. The word has been used admiringly by and about everyone from Margaret Thatcher to Nick Clegg to Tony Blair in relation to an array of policies. The word's meaning to voters, though, varies according to the voter and the context in which it is used. When applied to a Muslim in the present British and global context its connotations for many are sinister.

Moreover, the new Goldsmith attack in general ascribed to Khan characteristics ascribed to all Muslims by dedicated Muslim-haters and sought to create worries about him that some Londoners have about Muslims in general. Simply asking, "Who is Sadiq Khan?" directly questioned the Labour man's trustworthiness as an individual, encouraging suspicions about his true intentions, motivations and loyalties. Such doubts are daily raised about Muslims everywhere, not least in London after 7/7.

Goldsmith's team protested that it was merely and quite legitimately shining a light on what it regarded as inconsistencies in Khan's record as a politician. It was, though, beyond dispute that this assault on Khan struck exactly the chord its critics predicted with at least some people following the mayoral contest. Adam Bienkov, deputy editor and London specialist of the website Politics.co.uk, reported that a SadiqWatch video posted on the

Conservatives' Facebook page quickly attracted a number of unpleasant comments. One described Khan as "a dishonest Muslim" and a "cheap crook". Another complained: "The native population is being diluted on a horrendous scale." A third declared: "If Khan/Corbyn get in you can expect another 50 mosques in London, more extremists, no thank you there's too many already. Vote in the Tory candidate."

Labour widened its riposte to Goldsmith. Shadow employment minister and Islington South MP Emily Thornberry accused him and the Tories of "running a divisive and dog-whistling campaign – trying to turn London's communities against each other". This throwing of the word "divisive" back at Goldsmith underlined that Khan was determined to present himself as the true London candidate, the one who really knew the capital and personified its finest qualities. As 2015 drew to its end, the character of the two campaigns was taking human form: Khan, savvy, streetwise and not averse to a scrap versus Goldsmith, the courtly patrician who'd hired a heavy mob to do his fighting for him.

Four

January

The predictions of political commentators are often based as much on instincts as on stats. That doesn't mean those instincts can't be right, especially when they become a chorus that crosses ideological lines. As London returned to work after the festive break, pundits on the Economist, the New Statesman and the Daily Telegraph all anticipated a Khan victory. None put their money on Goldsmith.

At the Statesman, Stephen Bush described Goldsmith as "somewhat overrated" and thought Khan's candidacy had a "symbolic potency". The Telegraph's James Kirkup doubted that Goldsmith was "the exceptional Tory" needed to win Labour-leaning London and claimed that "some senior Tories" privately shared this view. He even questioned whether Conservatives as a whole yearned for Khan's defeat, as a Goldsmith win would lessen the chances of Corbyn leading Labour into the 2020 general election: "They'd never admit it in a thousand years, but if Mr Khan does indeed become mayor in May, George Osborne,

Boris Johnson and anyone else who wants to be Conservative prime minister in 2020 might quietly toast his victory."

The bookmakers agreed about Goldsmith's chances, shortening the odds on Khan over the Christmas period to make him favourite. New Year hostilities began against this backdrop. Khan began developing his characterisation of Goldsmith as a spoiled dilettante. The multi-millionaire was a "serial and habitual underachiever" he told the Sunday Times: "He never finishes anything he starts." The posh boy's *curriculum vitae* outside politics wasn't up to much either, according to the council estate kid: "He's somebody who before becoming a member of parliament has had one proper job, which was given to him by his uncle."

The next day, the first Monday of 2016, Khan told the Evening Standard of his plans for a four-year public transport fares freeze, including how he intended to make up for the £452m he said would be lost in fares revenue as a result. He gave Goldsmith a slap there too, reprising his remark about the gift of a "niche magazine" job and claiming that David Cameron "hasn't deemed him good enough even to be a junior minister, despite voting with the Tory whip more than nine times out of ten, including to dismantle London's NHS, cut tax credits and sell off affordable homes".

Goldsmith, though, had his own big announcement to make on the same day. It offered a completely different view of the most contentious parts of the Housing and Planning Bill Khan had challenged Goldsmith to oppose in his speech to the Labour conference. These followed Cameron announcing out of the blue during the general election campaign that if he won he would extend the legal right enjoyed by council house tenants to purchase their homes from their local authority at a heavily discounted price to people who rent from housing associations. The cost of this spreading of the "right-to-buy" - introduced by Margaret Thatcher in 1980 - to a whole new category of social housing occupants would be met by forcing councils to sell what was termed their "high value" housing when such properties became vacant, such as when tenants moved or died.

In theory, the money raised from such sales would fund councils building replacement homes for those they'd been forced to sell and also compensate housing associations for having to sell homes they owned for less than their market value. The Conservatives argued that this would both increase home ownership and finance the building of many more "affordable" homes of various kinds. Others did not share their confidence. The Confederation of British Industry and top drawer property consultants Jones Lang LaSalle said the measure would not address Britain's chronic housing shortage. The Institute for Fiscal

Studies, a highly respected independent research organisation, said it risked "a further depletion of the social housing stock" rather than an increase, with the loss particularly felt in expensive areas. London contains the most expensive areas in Britain. A leading spokesperson for the capital's business community described the Tory proposals as "bonkers".

This did not deter London's Tory MPs, including Goldsmith, from declining to oppose the Housing and Planning Bill. They argued that an amendment to it, which had Goldsmith's name attached, would end fears that huge sums raised from council house sales in London would be exported from the capital to subsidise housing association building elsewhere, and leave London even shorter of social and other forms of "affordable" housing than it already was. The amendment was designed to ensure that two new "affordable" homes of some kind would be built somewhere in London for every council house a borough was forced to sell. The government claimed that this would produce 10,000 units of housing on top of 50,000 resulting from other policy measures.

Under a joint byline in the Evening Standard, Cameron and Goldsmith described their approach as "radical" – presumably a good kind of radical rather than the variety Goldsmith's campaign had ascribed to Sadiq Khan – and wrote that their "mission for 2016 is to help Londoners of all incomes find a foothold on the housing ladder". Though hardly a surprise and with many details remaining obscure, the timing of its presentation to the public enabled Goldsmith to share the day's London coverage with his main rival.

He also hit back at Khan's criticism of his track record, telling BBC Radio London he had turned down a ministerial post shortly after entering parliament in 2010 and claiming that Khan had no record as a parliamentarian for co-operating with people outside his own party: "It is hard to see how that would work for four years under a Conservative government." Behold once more the Friend of Dave and George.

The start of 2016 also saw a further ushering of race and faith on to the scene alongside the already immoveable presence of Corbyn. Radio 4's Today programme, the national broadcaster's flagship morning show, was more interested in how close Khan was to his party leader or distant from him than anything he might offer the nation's capital. Goldsmith was pressed on the "radical and divisive" leaflet. He insisted it only pointed out that Labour under its new leader was radical, as in left-wing. He countered that Khan had played "the race card" when it "clearly and unambiguously does not apply".

Khan's team did not back down. It repeated its claim about the leaflet and described Goldsmith's campaign as "desperate". This might have seemed premature so early in the proceedings, had Khan not seemed to be making all the running. He was constructing a story about himself as the personification of the London of buzzing possibility: the big city that gave little people a chance; the London that had drawn Londoners to it from all over Britain and the world; the London that made Londoners feel pride. By comparison, Goldsmith's campaign seemed passive and dull. Though neither man excelled at broadcast media, Khan's appearances left a hallmark impression of hunger for the job, while Goldsmith came across as pleasant yet mildly aloof.

A new YouGov poll published on 7 January did not contradict such impressions. It found that Khan had entered 2016 in the lead, with 31% of respondents saying he'd be their choice as mayor compared with 24% who preferred Goldsmith – an increase of 1% since the end of November. This was statistically insignificant, but Khan had also improved his head-to-head rating against the Tory by a more substantial 4% to a hefty 10%. If that gap were real, how would it be closed?

*****

Goldsmith's campaign immediately reached for the Corbyn connection in an attempt to slow Khan down. For several months, the introduction of a new all-night service on the London Underground had been delayed by a dispute between the service's management and three of the unions representing its workers. When the latter announced plans to hold three one-day strikes over pay and rostering, it gave Goldsmith the chance to again depict Khan as the puppet of organised Labour and a menacing manifestation of "Jeremy Corbyn's Labour Party". Boris Johnson pitched in too, using the same formula.

Khan retaliated. His campaign released an image of a mock cv attached to a clipboard. An unflattering representation of the Tory's career record was punched out in impolite terms: appointed Ecologist editor by his uncle; a London MP who'd (apparently) said he was more comfortable in the country; allegedly "not good enough" to be a minister. Shortly before Christmas, Heathrow chairman Sir Nigel Rudd had made some choice remarks about Goldsmith: "He was left money by his daddy, he's never had a job other than a job given to him by his uncle, so what qualification has he got to do anything?" This rasping put down was reprised in the cod report. The "serial underachiever" jibe was repeated beneath a capitalised "rejected". If Khan was to be portrayed by Goldsmith as a fly operator, Goldsmith was to be branded a pampered failure by Khan.

Khan continued to accumulate flattering press coverage from unexpected sources. "In the race to become London mayor, one candidate seems to have a clear lead when it comes to courting the business community," reported the Financial Times. By then, Khan had visited the Federation of Small Businesses, the Institute of Directors, the London Chamber of Commerce and Industry, the City of London Corporation and London First, the body representing the capital's larger businesses and its universities. He'd told the Spectator he welcomed the fact that there were more than 140 billionaires living in London. "If you shut your eyes, it could be Peter Mandelson talking," observed his interviewer, a reference to one of Tony Blair's closest lieutenants.

There had been a New Labour flavour too to a speech Khan had made to the Resolution Foundation, a think tank concerned with the fortunes of people on low to middle incomes. His main announcement was his ambition to make London "the world's first Living Wage city" but the speech also painted a picture of a thriving London economy in which the interests of business and those of its lower paid were reconciled. He saw himself "building a coalition for shared prosperity" involving "working with business to increase productivity" by setting up a strategic body called Skills for Londoners, where boroughs and educators would work together to fill skills gaps more efficiently. His "inclusive prosperity" would tackle housing costs and also the price of childcare, often overlooked as a barrier to women in particular being part of the expensive city's workforce. For Khan, it was "a matter of both social justice and economic failure. He wanted to offer London business "a new compact". The Living Wage city would be created using "carrots, not sticks".

The Financial Times quoted an unnamed City figure making an unflattering comparison with Goldsmith: "Sadiq's been getting round and meeting people. Business leaders are coming away impressed." By contrast: "Zac's engagement has been less than impressive." The following day, the Daily Telegraph carried a scrupulously neutral interview with Khan, which, set among pages regularly graced by the bravura prose of Mayor Johnson, came across as warm and approving. "He is the left-leaning son of a bus driver who grew up on a council estate and nominated Jeremy Corbyn for Labour leader," it began: "But Sadiq Khan has used an interview with the Telegraph to make a direct pitch to Conservative voters to pick him as the next mayor of London over Tory Zac Goldsmith."

Khan got his big messages across: he would put aside party loyalties to stick up for London; he'd disagree with "Jeremy" if required, as he already did over airport capacity, new taxes on business and even over renewing the UK's Trident nuclear weapons programme. And, of course, on Muslim extremism: unlike Corbyn, he was very firmly in favour of shooting terrorists dead.

These pieces closely followed two insightful Conservative Home articles. Each betrayed anxieties about the prospects of the Tory candidate. Andrew Gimson, author of a friendly but illusion-less biography of Johnson, dwelt on the Labour candidate's enthusiasm for being "pro-everything: unions, business, the poor, the rich" and remarked that this "eagerness to please could get out of hand". But he ended by acknowledging the consistency of Khan's views on Muslim participation in British society. And he began by observing that, far from being "the insignificant little man" he thought Tessa Jowell's supporters had misjudged him as, Khan was turning out to be "a more formidable politician than I realised before writing this profile".

The other Conservative Home piece was written by the website's editor, Paul Goodman. Where Gimson acknowledged Khan's manifesting strengths as a politician, Goodman was moved to ask if Goldsmith was a politician at all. He contrasted him with the "focused, adaptable, on-message, risk-averse party political operator" that was Khan. "Zac is an eclectic, romantic, somewhat off-message, risk-taking individualist who doesn't always do what the whips tell him," Goodman wrote: "Being his own man, a conviction campaigner, unspun and a bit shy is part of his charm." He felt that most of the restiveness he'd detected among fellow Tories could be taken with a pinch of salt and that the Zac show was getting on the road. But even so:

> *"This few-holds-barred scrap for the mayoralty will be rather different from the civilised business of seeking re-election in his beautiful constituency. It will require Zac, without losing his freewheeling style, to keep working – 'that's what he needs to do: to show energy,' a senior London Tory mused aloud this week to me – 'and show discipline'."*

Conservatives had got their fairy tale candidate. But when would Sleeping Beauty wake?

*****

Goldsmith had, in fact, been working on his pitch, inconspicuous though this had been. Even the positive parts were negative in that they portrayed Khan as a threat against which the Tory would provide a stout defence. The Underground dispute provided an opportunity to use the ploy. "Help Zac to protect Londoners from Tube strikes," urged his Twitter feed, hailing Goldsmith's backing for the government's forthcoming Trade Union Bill, which would limit the ability of Underground workers to call strikes. As the Night Tube dispute dragged on, Tory campaigners leafleted stations.

At last, on the morning of 19 January, Goldsmith made a formal start on setting out his electoral stall. A press conference was called to announce to announce an "action plan for Greater London", a title which might have been designed to answer suggestions of lethargy and which in its use of the word "Greater" was undoubtedly aimed at suburban areas where Tory support was strongest.

For his location Goldsmith chose Croydon, with its changing social character and array of suburban concerns. The event was not a manifesto launch but a formal presentation of the candidate and his main themes. Four were given headline status, each of just two words: "more homes", "better transport", "cleaner air", "safer streets". Behind these lay more detailed messages, including some of manicured subtlety.

High up in a town centre building, Goldsmith was introduced by Gavin Barwell, MP for the most marginal of the borough's three constituencies, a government whip and a shrewd political operator. Goldsmith could be an insubordinate backbencher, he explained with a fondness he perhaps did not always feel in his capacity as parliamentary enforcer. Ah, but in a mayor, Barwell implied, such recalcitrance could be a sterling quality.

Rainfall fugged the backdrop window and its view of tower blocks under construction as

Goldsmith stepped up to the podium. He wore a dark suit, white shirt and a mossy green tie with flecks. He thanked those present - party supporters and selected journalists - for turning out on such an inclement day before introducing himself with a caressing irony that admitted to potential weaknesses: "I might be wrong, ah, but I think my Labour rival may have mentioned a few times that I was dealt a good hand in life. He's right. I was."

With that glancing reference, the small embarrassment of a massive mound of wealth was vanished from the room like a steaming dog turd whisked from a Persian rug by a discreet servant. Suddenly, Goldsmith wasn't talking about an unearned personal fortune at all. Instead, his "good hand" was characterised as a colourful genealogy. "I can't do that thing that politicians so often do, when they say they were the first in their family to consider a role in formal politics," he disclosed to his tame audience with a mime of diffident regret.

Goldsmith met Khan's life story of urban grit with tales of timeless English eccentricity. He spoke of his father's father, turned against by his Suffolk constituents. Uncle Edward got a mention as founder of the forerunner of the Green Party, and there was his dad, of course, the late Sir James, depicted in Croydon not as a ruthless corporate predator but as the leader of "a renegade political party calling for an EU referendum". Goldsmith even name-checked his erstwhile brother-in-law

Imran Khan, former captain of the Pakistan cricket team, who had ambitions to become that country's leader.

But this pedigree was, Goldsmith insisted, no reason for complacency. In his one allusion to his wealth he said: "That hand I was dealt, I have always been utterly determined to play it well. To campaign for the things that matter, to challenge those things that I felt were wrong. And I've been involved in real politics far longer than I've been a politician." Goldsmith may have inherited a feather bed but he wasn't going to lie around in it all day.

There followed a litany of indirect rebuttals to charges Khan had laid. The Ecologist was portrayed as "a down and out magazine" that he'd "transformed into a fighting force". But "real politics" were possible as an MP too, Goldsmith explained. He'd become one because he wanted to do more than shout from the sidelines about problems. He wanted to "fix things" and was proud of what he'd achieved "for my own community" such as "securing funds for Kew Gardens and keeping the use of Richmond Park free".

He'd never seen the job as "a springboard for something bigger," he insisted. "I willingly gave up any chance of promotion to government by voting always with my conscience, even when that set me against my own party," he continued, with a confirming aside to Barwell. "My Labour opponent thinks lack of promotion in politics is a sign of under achievement," he went on. But that barb, he maintained, was in truth a damning commentary on Khan's priorities.

These were, Goldsmith contended, as compromised as his were pure: "I won't change my mind with the political winds...I will always deliver what I promise. But there is one candidate in this election who won't – Jeremy Corbyn's candidate. Sadiq Khan is a caricature machine politician." Citing Khan's about-face over Heathrow and his wooing of both City bosses and union chiefs, he dubbed him "the sort of politician who justifies peoples' mistrust in politics". He predicted that London under a Mayor Khan would be used as "an experiment for Corbyn's radical policies".

Here was the most formal framing yet of Khan as the unprincipled instrument of a dastardly Corbynite masterplan. Yet there were grounds for doubting its veracity, its plausibility and its likely efficacy. The suggestion that the Labour candidate was a puppet of the Labour leader bent on using the capital as a dry run for a deranged national agenda was flatly contradicted by the nature and organisation of Khan's campaign. From the start, it had been entirely separate from Corbyn's office in Westminster. At least one party staff member who'd worked for Ed Miliband and was now working for Khan regarded himself as blessed, like a shipwreck survivor washed up on a sun-kissed shore with the words "refugees welcome" written in the sand.

Acting on advice from one of the wiser members of his team, Corbyn had asked Karen Buck, the much-respected and non-Corbynite MP for Westminster North, if she would consider chairing Khan's campaign as a way of providing some light touch liaison. With Eltham MP Clive Efford brought in as Buck's deputy chair, the arrangement was agreed and did its job. Otherwise, Khan's campaign functioned entirely autonomously. And, contrary to Goldsmith's assertions, any future Mayor Khan would be still more independent of the leader of Her Majesty's loyal opposition. He would be the most powerful Labour politician in the country. Corbyn would have no dominion over him at all. The mayoralty is not set up that way.

At the same time, there were grounds for questioning if trying to yoke Khan to Corbyn in the public mind would have the effect Goldsmith desired. Although the Khan camp was plainly worried that it might, there was no particular evidence that Corbyn was dragging Khan down, at least among Labour supporters. Fragments of national polls, including on the Syria issue, and post-September borough by-election results suggested that although Labour support had slipped in most of the country, it was holding up quite well in the capital. It appeared that Goldsmith's "Khan-Corbyn experiment" misrepresentation was, like the rest of his strategy, designed principally to put a chill in suburban Tory hearts.

Most of the rest of the Croydon address comprised riffs already familiar to the cognoscenti, if not yet to the electorate at large: Goldsmith was friends with Cameron but would not be his flunky; he would build on the legacy of the "force of nature" and "fantastic mayor" that was "Boris"; he would cherish London's greenery. The most enlightening passage concerned housing policy, the issue topping Londoners' list of concerns. Goldsmith reprised previous lines on estate regeneration and his "Londoners first" stance on new homes built on public land, and he again hailed the "two-for-one" Housing and Planning Bill amendment, for which he'd taken credit. His closing words on housing were crystal clear: "We will have succeeded when more young people on average salaries get the keys to their first home."

Later that day, two of the Tube unions called off their strike plans while the third looked to be getting round to it. That issue was dead for the time being. Goldsmith, though, was at last coming alive, an ethereal, patrician presence sensing the yearnings of his natural allies, feeling the pulse of their anxieties and softly urging them to be afraid, be afraid, be afraid.

*****

The first hustings of the campaign took place on 28 January in the sumptuous 400-seat Sheikh Zayed lecture theatre of the London School of Economics, which sits between Kingsway and Lincoln's Inn Fields. The location and the institution are steeped in several histories, some very old, others new. The Fields, laid out in the 1630s, form London's largest public square. A scene from Bleak House is set there, a traitor lost his head there and wealthy lawyers have set up shop there down the decades. Rough sleepers have gathered there too. Local Muslims have fed them during Ramadan.

The LSE was founded in 1895 by the Fabian Society, that eminent think tank Sadiq Khan would chair more than a century later. The lecture theatre, opened in 2008, is named after Sheikh Zayed, the late ruler of the United Arab Emirates, due to the Zayed Centre, a think tank he funded, donating £2.5m towards its cost. This was not without controversy: Harvard University had returned a similar donation, claiming that the Zayed Centre had helped with the promotion of anti-Semitic ideas.

Into this grand auditorium stepped Goldsmith, Khan and three other candidates for mayor: Siân Berry, representing the Green Party; Peter Whittle of the United Kingdom Independence Party (Ukip) and Liberal Democrat Caroline Pidgeon. All three were also competing for seats on the London Assembly.

These come in two types. Fourteen of the 25 are for members representing constituencies – sometimes called "super constituencies" – comprising two or three borough areas and are decided by individual first-past-the-post contests. Only the two biggest parties have ever won the constituency seats. The additional eleven seats are assigned through a form of proportional representation designed to give the smaller parties a look-in. Those parties winning more than 5% of the total in this part of the assembly election are in with a chance. The allocations are then made by means of a mathematical formula called modified d'Hondt. Berry, Whittle and Pidgeon were at the top of their respective parties' lists of candidates to become assembly members in this way.

The event's organiser was London Tomorrow, a "thought leadership initiative" set up by the London Chamber of Commerce and Industry to look into the capital's future. Colin Stanbridge, the Chamber's chief executive, was in the chair. Lots had been drawn. Goldsmith, who had just turned 41, stepped up to the podium first.

"London has boomed under Boris Johnson," he began and explained that he wanted to "take that extraordinary success story" and "translate it – I want to make it work for everyone in London". He ran through his action plan list and warned: "It's easy when you're running up to an election to make all kinds of promises, but the issue is who can deliver the promises they make." Mentioning no names. "If London backs me on May 5th, in 96 days' time, I will make Greater London greater still," he said.

Whittle was up next up: TV producer, film critic, royalist and dapper hope of a reactionary populism rallied around a Eurosceptic flag. Though weaker in London than elsewhere in the country and winning just twelve London council seats in 2014, the party had nonetheless secured 8.1% of the overall London vote share at the general election, the third highest after Labour and the Conservatives.

The round of applause was generous. Whittle, his party's spokesperson on culture, was pleasantly surprised: "Thank you, ladies and gentlemen for that clap. Most unexpected." The ladies and gentlemen laughed. "This *is* the LSE," was Whittle's reasoned ad-lib. Left-wing agitation was another strand of the neighbourhood's history, one he seemed warily conscious of. "I'm a born and bred Londoner, like my father before me and my grandparents," he said. He was born in Peckham and now lived in Woolwich. He felt his roots were the bedrock of his identity: "I don't know whether you know what I mean, but when you talk about being a Londoner it's something which actually forms my whole character. I look at the world in a particular way."

He complimented London Tomorrow for its prescriptions on infrastructure, describing these as crucial to the "machine" that is London's economy. But quality of life was crucial too: "I think this is something which in the last 10 or 20 years we have seriously neglected." This led him on to the two ways he felt sure he would be different from all the others on the panel. One was his position on population growth, which he approached somewhat obliquely: "You've got to say this is something which, as mayor, I would want to address." Secondly: "I can say sincerely that I am the only candidate here tonight who believes that London has an extremely exciting future – *business in London has a very exciting future* - outside of the EU."

Berry went third. She had run for mayor before, in 2008, finishing fourth. With her slight build and long, blonde hair she had inevitably been dubbed "the green goddess". Berry had spent the intervening years writing, campaigning and getting elected to Camden Council. Now 41, she had become a seasoned and confident politician. "I'm here because I want London to succeed, but the way it succeeds is important too," she stressed: "The concentration of wealth in a few hands isn't good for our city." Neither was: "The concentration of commerce in a few large businesses." Her view was that helping smaller enterprises would create "a more diverse and resilient economy for London". She argued that: "The power of our ideas is that they look to the long term – not just to the next election. With a Green mayor, London's future and its future success will be in safe hands."

Then came Khan. "Good evening," he began: "London is the greatest city in the world. But we're at a crossroads. And if we don't act now, it could be too late." Yes, there was danger: "Londoners are being priced out, due to the housing crisis and the next generation are missing out on the opportunities that me and my family had." He recounted his family story: the council home; the state schools; the university place for him and all but one of his siblings, who qualified as a motor mechanic - "the most successful of the Khans," quipped the Labour man. "London needs a mayor with the experience, with the values and with the vision to put us on the right track," he declared.

Finally came the candidate with by far the most experience of City Hall politics. Pidgeon, 43, had already been a member of the London Assembly – an AM – for two terms. Like Berry and Whittle, she was hoping to finish third behind Goldsmith and Khan. The Lib Dems had been squeezed into fourth by the Greens in 2012 and had a miserable general election: in London, the party had retained only one seat out of the seven they had previously held. On Pidgeon rested their hopes of a comeback.

Neat and determined, she majored on pedigree and practicality, presenting herself as a low ego doer, someone who grafts hard and gets things done about community policing, air quality and most particularly transport, a subject on which she was spokesperson for her two-strong assembly group. "For me, the way our city works is personal," she said: "Not because I'm involved in its politics but because I'm one of London's ordinary citizens too." She was a working mother who knew first hand about the costs and complications of childcare. She'd been a housing campaigner for more than 20 years, including as a councillor in Southwark. She had policies for addressing those issues and for targeted public transport fare cuts. "This election is wide open," she insisted: "The power is in your hands."

The debate had a preliminary feel as the contestants circled each other like strangers thrown together at a cocktail party. The tone was civil, the disagreements polite. The marking out of territory was subtle and, on the part of the two frontrunners, no doubt at least a little mindful of the benefit each might accrue from being more appealing to supporters of the other candidates than his chief rival. No one had ever won a London Mayor election on first preference votes alone and none seemed likely to in 2016. Therefore, the destination of Lib Dem, Green and Ukip second preferences were going to be of interest to Goldsmith and Khan.

That day, it had been announced that the commissioner of the Metropolitan Police, Sir Bernard Hogan-Howe, had been given a one-year extension to his contract. The news was a reminder of the power London Mayors can exert over London's most senior police officer. Even before the Mayor's Office for Policing and Crime was established in 2012, formally making him directly accountable to voters for police performance, Boris Johnson had surprised many by as good as forcing the then commissioner Sir Ian Blair to resign. Sir Ian's successor Sir Paul Stephenson hadn't lasted very long, stepping down after attracting criticism for having as an adviser a former senior executive of the News of the World newspaper, which was under investigation for illegal phone hacking.

Hogan-Howe had headed the Merseyside service before becoming the top dog in British policing. Johnson's decision to give him job security for only the next twelve months was being seen as enabling his successor as mayor to get the measure of his top cop before deciding to extend his contract further. How did the five candidates rate Sir Bernard?

Pidgeon, deputy chair of the assembly's police and crime committee, thought him the best commissioner she'd worked with, apart from his supporting the purchase of those useless water cannon. Berry liked Hogan-Howe too. Whittle said he'd been impressed by him and added that he thought it would be nice if neighbourhood police officers came from the areas they patrolled, although he didn't want to seem "too rose-tinted or nostalgic". Goldsmith? "I'm a big fan of Bernard Hogan-Howe," he said. Khan's response was cuter. Making a swift raid behind enemy lines, he praised Johnson's thinking on the one-year extension before expressing alarm about the levels of knife crime, gang crime and offences against women.

He then took a jab at the effects of cuts to police budgets, saying it was vital to ensure that "we have bobbies back on the beat". This Whittle-like assertion was topped off with a wisecrack. When Stanbridge remarked that Hogan-Howe's future employment prospects looked to be good, Khan said: "He's probably listening in."

The remark may have been more loaded than it seemed. In 2008 it had emerged that Thames Valley Police had secretly recorded conversations between Khan and a Tooting resident named Babar Ahmad, who was in prison and resisting extradition to the United States to face terrorism charges. Khan's hustings speech contained the plainest law and order language. His past connection with Ahmad might have been one reason why. So might a guide he'd produced when a lawyer for those considering legal action against the police. So might his call in January 2014, when shadow Justice Secretary and following the inquest into the death of Mark Duggan, for the police's use of stop-and-search powers to be re-thought. So might his own criticism at that time of the Met's water cannon purchase.

The remainder of the evening was significant mainly for another point of unanimity. Everyone wanted to protect the green belt. Unlike during the Tory selection hustings back in September, Goldsmith offered no caveat about possibly reopening the discussion about it if London's population continued to boom: "I'm absolutely on the record as saying that the green belt is a black line. You simply do not build on it." All that had changed was that the autumn's "red line" was now of a different shade. So it was clear by the end that the five would-be mayors were unanimous about two things: that our green belt and our policemen are wonderful. There was a winning sign off from Whittle. He revealed that he is gay.

*****

At the end of the month, the Goldsmith campaign received a gift. It took the form of a Transport for London briefing note supplied to BBC London's transport correspondent Tom Edwards. The note said that the four-year public transport fares freeze Khan had proposed would deprive TfL not of £452m but of £1.9bn - over four times the figure claimed by Khan. A TfL official told Edwards that the difference was largely due to Khan failing to take into account that overall income from fares was projected to increase over that period, partly because population increase - projected to soar from a recently-reached record 8.6 million to 10 million by 2030 - would mean more and more passengers making use of the buses, the Underground and so on, and partly because the new, high capacity, Crossrail east-west rail link would start coming into service from 2018.

Goldsmith seized on the gift with understandable glee. Khan simply denied that the TfL figures represented what the organisation really believed about his plans. Action had flared on one of the key campaign battlegrounds and offered Goldsmith the chance to deploy one of his favourite pieces of campaign artillery: the charge that Khan as mayor would be the dodgy instrument of Corbyn lunacy.

Five

February

Three weeks after Goldsmith went south to Croydon to launch his action plan, Khan went west to do something similar in the town of Isleworth. This was home territory insofar as the previous year Labour had gained the parliamentary seat of Brentford and Isleworth, which lies in the Labour-run borough of Hounslow. But it was also far from Labour's Inner London heartlands. A signal was being sent about Khan caring for the suburbs too.

The venue was West Thames College, a further and higher education institution where 6,500 students study each year. It's rated good by education watchdog Ofsted. Its alumni include the late Freddie Mercury. It has won awards for equality and diversity, though not every local resident celebrated. "You can't miss it," said a fellow in a curious hat who gave directions. He broke the reasons for this gently, white man to white man, in a consoling tone: "Outside, there will be, how shall I put it? Leftovers from the British Empire."

Khan's launch was staged in a communal part of an airy modern building before a seated crescent of Labour supporters and the half dozen journalists who'd been invited. He stepped up to the podium in a midnight blue suit and a crisp, white, open-necked shirt. Behind him flowed his campaign branding: Khan photographed against a Square Mile background above a ribbon of four intertwining colours shaped like the Isle of Dogs loop of the Thames. The slogan read: "Sadiq Khan For London."

Khan said: "London is the greatest city in the world. But we're at a crossroads. Many of the things that make our city so amazing are at real risk and if we don't act *now* it could be too late. Ordinary Londoners are being priced out of *our* city, pushed further and further out by the Tory housing crisis and the increasing cost of commuting, ending London's wonderful social mix that's *lasted* for centuries."

His assessment of risk also embraced social mobility. "The next generation of Londoners are missing out on the opportunities that our city gave me," he said: "The hand they're dealt at birth is increasingly defining their chances of success in life. That's not the kind of city I want London to be. That's why I'm so determined to win this election for *all* Londoners."

His delivery was deliberate, perhaps in recognition of a need to slow his usual rapid diction. The result was slightly mannered: a storybook note to the opening line; a little too much stress on that "all", that "our", that "now"; a hard-pedalled "lasted" that left the clinching "centuries" underplayed. But the key messages were sent to the onlooking TV cameras and reporters. Khan's London, the Labour man declared, would deliver modern "affordable" transport; it would be stronger, fairer, safer and greener; the "Tory housing crisis" would be "fixed".

This performance filmed and taped, Khan joined the journalists for a 15-minute huddle. The fares freeze dispute was on their minds. His checklist answer was to hand. But wouldn't he need to recast Transport for London as a different kind of public body to make his numbers add up? Would TfL, a power in its own right, cooperate? Khan said there was "no alternative" to this and that the organisation's new commissioner Mike Brown understood that it would have to become "more slimline" and geared to "sweat its assets more". He revealed that he was looking forward to chairing the TfL board, perhaps mentioning this to scotch a rumour that Ken Livingstone might be installed in the role.

Khan was asked about the redevelopment of TfL land for homes. He wanted this accelerated to take in less expensive, Outer London areas: "TfL has said there's plenty of land in zones 3 to 6 which is coming on stream shortly. Why don't we use that land to build affordable homes?" His question raised others. Already, TfL had teamed up with property giant Capital and Counties in the demolition of the historic Earls Court exhibition centre, which had stood on TfL-owned land. It was to be replaced by a 1,200-dwelling "village" containing no "affordable" homes at all.

A list of further "prime central" sites and potential developer partners was due to be announced. TfL's director of commercial development had said that exploiting the financial potential of TfL sites "has to be our top priority". Was there not, therefore, a conflict between maximising revenue from TfL sites and maximising the number of "affordable" homes built on them? "That's an important reason why Londoners should vote for me, not the other guy," Khan said, unfazed: "Because the other guy is continuity. I want to have change."

Crews from BBC London and ITV London News had set up shop on a walkway above. The former's political editor Tim Donovan pressed Khan further about homes on TfL land. How many "affordable" ones could get built on it each year? "That depends on how much land we can free up from TfL," Khan said. There should be "at least 50% genuinely affordable homes" on it for low social rents or for part-buy, part-rent "shared ownership" whereby the purchaser owns a portion of the home. Khan threw in some detail: "From the modelling we've done, we think the deposit you would need to purchase one of these shared ownership homes would be £5,200. The rental part of the scheme would be £400 cheaper than you're paying under current schemes."

Donovan pointed out that London's housing associations, which build the majority of "affordable" homes in the capital and would therefore probably build those on TfL land, need the income from the rented part of shared ownership schemes. If that income were to decrease, how would housing associations make up the difference? Did Khan intend to subsidise them in some way, and if so how? Khan said he was looking forward to "going into partnership" with housing associations and also private developers to put his plans into effect. He mentioned Camden Council, which, in partnership with a commercial firm, had pioneered building homes for market sale on its own land in order to subside the building of new council and shared ownership homes. "If Camden can do that on land it owns, I think the mayor can do that on land he owns," Khan said.

Donovan still wanted responses to his numbers question and his rent subsidy point. But Khan said: "The big difference between me and Boris Johnson and me and Zac Goldsmith is there won't be a fire sale of this land if I am the mayor. What London can't afford is mayors selling off this land to the highest bidders."

In fact, TfL had long since made clear its intention to retain the freehold of its land in order to ensure a long-term income stream from it.

Khan's argument would have been more accurately applied to chunks of the Metropolitan Police estate that were being sold off by Stephen Greenhalgh.

For the Labour candidate, though, such matters were not at all the point of his talking to Donovan. The point was to say to TV viewers things like this: "Voting for me will ensure you can fulfil your dream of being a home owner, that you can afford to live in London on a rent [and] you can live in the city you've been born and raised in."

And this: "It is a travesty that homes are sold off plan to investors in the Middle East and Asia."

And this: "If you've been renting for more than five years in London, you will go to the head of the queue. It will be first dibs for Londoners."

Later inquiries revealed a broad journalistic consensus: "He sticks to his messages like glue."

*****

The following evening came the second major hustings of the campaign. The Evening Standard hired the handsome headquarters of the Royal Geographical Society in Kensington Gore next to the Royal Albert Hall for the occasion. They invited the same five candidates as had appeared at the LSE event – Goldsmith, Khan, Berry, Pidgeon and Whittle - plus two more. One was Sophie Walker, a former business journalist representing the

Women's Equality Party. The other was George Galloway of the Respect Party, pretty much representing just himself.

Galloway personified a small part of the mayoral fight's potential to become personally astringent and subside into a mire of religion and ethnicity. Aged 61, he had previously been a Labour politician of some stature and charisma. Born in Dundee, he had, in 1981, become the youngest ever chair of the Scottish Labour Party and was general secretary of the London-based, international anti-poverty charity War on Want until elected as Labour MP for a seat in Glasgow in 1987. Brought up in a poor family amid Marxist ideas, Galloway took inspiration as a teenager from icon of the Cuban revolution Che Guevara. That admiration outlasted his Labour Party membership, which was ended in 2003. Galloway was found guilty by the party's National Executive Committee on four counts out of five of bringing it into disrepute by the way he had expressed his opposition to British involvement in the Iraq War and expelled.

The Respect Party had been formed the following year, its name an acronym for respect, equality, socialism, peace, environmentalism, community and trade unionism. At the 2005 general election, Galloway had taken revenge on Labour by depriving it of the constituency of Bethnal Green and Bow in Respect's name. The key to this triumph in a previously solid Labour seat had been a coalition of fellow leftists and Muslim activist groups attracted by Galloway's long-standing support for the Palestinian side of the Israel-Palestine conflict and his stance on Iraq. The Labour candidate he vanquished was Oona King, subsequent backer of Khan. King is half Jewish. She claimed afterwards to have been subjected to "one of the dirtiest campaigns we have ever seen in British politics" and said she had endured frequent anti-Semitic abuse on the streets. "I was fairly shocked by the levels to which it sank," she said.

Abandoning Bethnal Green, Galloway fought a neighbouring, more difficult East End seat for Respect in the 2010 general election, finishing third behind Labour and the Conservative runner-up. In 2012 he'd spectacularly overturned another Labour majority at a by-election in Bradford West with the support of Muslim voters of Pakistani descent, but that electoral high point preceded a string of personal and political lows. A few months after the sensational Bradford result, Respect co-founder Salma Yaqoob had left the party, saying she'd had to make a choice between "standing up for the rights of women" and her admiration for Galloway's "anti-imperialist stances". This had followed remarks made by Galloway about rape: "Not everybody needs to be asked prior to each insertion."

Galloway strongly denies any accusation that he harbours prejudices against Jews. However, his strong criticisms of Israel and gift for populist oratory inspire deep dislike among the 150,000 Jewish Londoners. In December 2014 he was violently attacked and injured in a London street by a recent convert to Judaism who called him an "anti-Semitic little man". Defending Bradford West in 2015, Galloway accused his Labour challenger Naz Shah of lying about the age she'd been when she'd married a cousin in Pakistan, a union she claimed had been forced on her when she was just 15. The accusation was strongly denied and supporting documents produced. Galloway lost Bradford West by an even larger majority than he'd won it by. He may not have helped himself by hinting prior to the vote that the London mayoral crown had caught his eye.

Respect had long since become a case study in the British far left's enduring gift for self-parodic, self-destructive splits. At the start of 2016 the Spectator reported that in 2014 Respect had had just 630 members nationally and assets of £1,947. The party had effectively become a vehicle for Galloway's public persona and global worldview. This was part of the backdrop against which Galloway had launched his mayoral bid. Another was Corbyn's ascent to the Labour Party leadership. The size of Galloway's personality had secured him some media coverage, which he'd made use of to get two main points across.

The first of these was that he was in intimate communication with Corbyn's leadership team. This was perfectly believable. When Galloway had been a Labour MP, he and Corbyn had been allies in parliament, implacably opposed to almost every policy of Tony Blair. He'd told the Sunday Times that Guardian columnist Seumas Milne, who had been granted leave from the paper to become the Labour leader's executive director of strategy and communications, was his "closest friend" with whom he'd "spoken almost daily for 30 years". Asked at a public meeting in Walthamstow whether Corbyn would be more pleased by a victory for him or for Khan, he'd dodged the question with a jest: "If I was Jeremy, I'd want to me to win."

Even when made back in November this claim had looked a little thin. Corbyn had already expressed his disapproval of Galloway's tactics against Naz Shah, telling the New Statesman he'd found them "appalling" and "shocking". Subsequently, London Labour MP Dawn Butler, chair of the women's parliamentary Labour Party, had written witheringly against any suggestion that Galloway be readmitted to Labour. She said she had been assured by Corbyn that he was "not in favour of letting Galloway back in". None of this deterred Galloway. "If you're looking for a Corbyn in this election, it's me," he'd told his audience in Walthamstow.

Galloway's second message, complementing the first, was that he held Sadiq Khan in contempt. In a string of glowing tributes he'd called him "a very boring man", a "flip-flop merchant", a "product of the Blairite machine", an accomplice in Blair era "crimes and blunders" and an "unprincipled speak-your-weight machine" who "went into what can only be described as a swoon over kissing the queen's hand". He seemed unaware of Khan's disagreements with Tony Blair over Iraq or that it was Gordon Brown who had promoted him from the backbenches. Galloway had told the Standard that the Labour man had erred when meeting the monarch by holding the Koran "in his left hand" and that this "wasn't missed by people who care about these things". He'd named Khan rather than Goldsmith as his prime target: "It's me versus Sadiq Khan for the centre left vote."

Following his street assault, Galloway had worn a fedora to cover his head wounds. Priding himself on his sartorial flair, he had continued to sport it after they had healed. The hat had become integral to the Galloway brand. It was firmly in place for the Standard hustings. Its wearer's penchant for a rhetorical flourish was also in conspicuous evidence.

In his opening statement he climbed aboard what he termed "the elephant in the room" and named this beast as "the overwhelming possibility of a Paris-style terrorist attack on London". Galloway pronounced himself to be "in the best position to prevent it and to respond to it if, God forbid, it should happen". His reasoning? He'd opposed the war in Iraq, which meant his understanding of the terrorist phenomenon was deeper. His solution? A law and order one: "If I'm mayor, we will have the police numbers, the police will have the weapons they need to defend us. And if terrorists come to harm us, then our police will shoot them, lawfully, dead." He then adapted a catch phrase coined by Blair in relation to crime: "I'm tough on terrorism and I'm tough on the causes of terrorism too." He said the government's Prevent strategy for combatting radicalisation needed improving, insisting: "I'm the man to lead it."

Thereafter, Galloway reverted to his two-track basic strategy of praising Corbyn and abusing Khan. After Khan expressed pride that his campaign was supported to the tune of £47,000 by trade unions, Galloway accused him of "picking their pockets" and of insulting bus drivers in a Sunday Times interview. The article in question had been headlined: "No offence, but I'm too clever to be a bus driver." This misrepresented what Khan was quoted in the interview as having said, which was as follows:

> "My dad was never embarrassed of being a bus driver, but it was clear, in a non-arrogant way, that he was better educated.

My parents wanted, again not in an arrogant way, but they wanted their children to do better than them. I don't mean this as a discourtesy to bus drivers."

So Khan had not described himself as being too clever to be a bus driver at all. Rather, he had spoken about his father having had an education that might have enabled him to secure a job requiring higher qualifications than were needed to drive a bus. He had stressed in the process that his father had not considered his job to be beneath him but had wanted his children get better ones. It wasn't the first time Galloway had deploying the misleading headline against Khan. After he'd done so before, the Independent's Andy McSmith had observed: "Nowhere is [Khan] quoted as saying he was 'too clever' to drive a bus; the phrase was obviously concocted by the headline writer. And I think Galloway is clever enough to have worked that out."

Galloway was also clever enough to give the Standard the sort of headline it might have been hoping for when it invited him. He said of Khan: "Since the day and hour that Jeremy Corbyn was elected leader, he has stabbed him in the back, in the front, in the side, and I for one ask everyone who supports Corbyn to vote for me, first preference in the election for London Mayor." Khan reacted to this with a display of amused tolerance:

he was sorry George felt that way and wondered archly if his supporters would favour him with their second preferences. He also advised Corbyn to "start talking to those people who disagree with you".

This too was reported by the Standard. And a case could be made for both men having gained from the encounter: for Galloway it was self-publicity, his political oxygen and avenue to future income through television and other media avenues; for Khan it reprised his insistence on his autonomy from Corbyn, which Galloway's insults helped to underline. Verbal hostility from the man in the hat appeared unlikely to hamper Khan's progress. Far more serious challenges were soon to come.

*****

For many months, since long before he became the Labour candidate, Khan's campaign had been anticipating newspaper stories claiming that Khan had "links" with Islamic extremists. Tales of scary Muslims represent good business for the news industry. The word "links" is invaluable for justifying them, a handy tool when implying a great deal about nothing much at all.

On 7 February an "extremist links" article appeared in the Sunday Times, the paper that had already brought the world the misleading bus driver headline about Khan. It said that in 2004 and 2005, before becoming an MP, Khan had been to four meetings organised by a group called Stop The Political Terror and that the group had enjoyed the support of a prominent jihadi propagandist, since deceased.

A spokesperson for Khan's campaign said that Khan had attended a number of events during that period in connection with opposing the extradition treaty between the United Kingdom and the United States, which would enable British citizens to be taken to the US and tried there for breaches of US law even if their alleged offences had been committed in the UK. It was this arrangement that Babar Ahmad had been fighting when Khan visited him in jail during the same period as the Stop Political Terror events had taken place.

The following week, the same newspaper reported that between 2004 and 2013 Khan had several times "spoken alongside" and "repeatedly shared a platform with" a Muslim cleric called Suliman Gani "even though Gani has called women 'subservient' to men" and had condemned homosexuality and gay marriage. This, the paper said, amounted to Khan "associating with extremists".

On 12 February, an "extremist links" story appeared in the Evening Standard, spread across two pages. Its headline proclaimed: "Exposed:

Sadiq Khan's family links to extremist organisation."
Beneath this banner it was "revealed" that Khan's
sister had once been married to a man who'd made
a speech in Trafalgar Square in 1997, apparently
criticising non-Muslim societies and advocating
Islamic ones. Wisely, the article quoted the man in
question, now a partner in a prestigious law firm,
describing his views at that time as regrettable
and naïve. He had divorced Khan's sister in 2011.
A spokesperson for Khan said he'd had no contact
with the man for ten years. Such was the extent of
the "links" in question.

Four days later, the Daily Mail was able to
"reveal" that Khan had spoken at an event in 2008
called the Global Unity and Peace festival organised
and broadcast by satellite television station the
Islam Channel. Most of the article drew attention
to the fact that while Khan had been speaking
one person in a large and packed auditorium had
waved what was described as "the black flag of
jihad". Also shown was a distant image of a woman
waving, according to the Mail, "what appears to be
a white version of the flag".

Fortified by these flag-wavers, the article felt
able to assert that, "Khan gave his support to
groups linked to extremism" and that his praise
of the emerging Islamic financial sector, the main
subject of his speech, would "raise concerns about
his intentions for the City of London if he is elected
mayor". It did not mention that other MPs had

spoken at the same event in subsequent years, including the then deputy prime minister Nick Clegg (Liberal Democrat) and the then attorney general Dominic Grieve (Conservative). In 2013, the festival had received a message of support from another prominent Tory. It read:

> "I am delighted to send a message of support to the organisers and attendees at the Global Peace & Unity Event. This hugely significant event in London does much to promote global cohesion across all communities; it increases understanding and encourages dialogue throughout the Muslim community and beyond... My best wishes once again and I hope this event is a huge success."

The Tory in question was Boris Johnson, who had been quite a champion of Islamic finance as mayor, even launching a World Islamic Economic Forum event to encourage investment in London. Adam Bienkov wrote:

> "While not a single one of these figures is attacked, or even mentioned by the Mail in their piece, Khan is for some reason singled out and condemned for his appearance at the [Global Peace and Unity] conference. So what is it about Khan that merits such

attention? Is it his views? This can hardly be the case given that Khan has been a vocal opponent of religious extremism for years. Could it be his prominence? Again this seems highly unlikely given that more senior politicians such as Boris have been given a pass. Surely the only viable explanation is that he's a senior Labour politician who happens to be Muslim."

Bienkov also wondered what lay behind this sudden cluster of stories:

"While no spokesperson for Zac Goldsmith has publicly commented on them, his campaign have highlighted them through their "Sadiq Watch" website. It also seems a remarkable coincidence that so many different papers could have suddenly all unearthed such similar stories at exactly the same time."

He concluded that there was plenty of scope for Goldsmith to take issue with Khan on straightforward matters of policy:

"Goldsmith should now concentrate on those and publicly distance himself from any further attempt to label Khan an "extremist" or any further attempt to whip

*up prejudice against somebody who could
soon become London's first Muslim mayor."*

No such distancing occurred.

*****

In the midst of all this, Transport for London
commissioner Mike Brown made an appearance
before the full London Assembly. He was closely
questioned by Labour AM and transport expert Val
Shawcross about the £1.9bn cost put on Khan's four
year fares freeze plan in the briefing note supplied
to BBC London's Tom Edwards. Brown said this
figure was, in fact, for the five-year period of TfL's
most recent business plan, rather than the four
years of a mayoral term. He also said that Khan's
figure of £452m was "perfectly understandable"
but that there were "different assumptions that
underpin different numbers".

Brown explained that TfL's figure assumed
that fares would in future be rising by inflation
as measured by the retail price index plus 1%. If
inflation as measured against the RPI remained at
1% TfL would lose an annual 2% increase in fares
each year for four years as a result of a freeze.
By that calculation, said Brown, the figure would
be £900m. However, he went on to say that TfL's
figure did not assume that RPI would stay at 1%

but that it would actually rise to 1.9% in 2017 and to 3.5% in 2018, 2019 and 2020. It was from these assumptions that the £1.9bn figure was derived. Shawcross challenged them, saying they were far higher than those of the Bank of England, which measures inflation differently. She added that, in any case, the TfL business plan was out of date. Brown acknowledged that TfL was highly adept at protecting its budget.

These detailed exchanges about compli-cated numbers were illuminating and did not go unre-ported. But in the end the electorate would make its choice about fares and much else on the basis of which candidate it thought most credible. Both Khan and Goldsmith were now deeply immersed in the battle for voters' trust and the focus was very much on Khan. Goldsmith could add TfL's brief-ing note to the "extremist links" barrage of his media allies - the Muslim Test exactingly applied. On transport, Khan had his life story as a defence: he was the bus driver's son who would make sure Londoners would pay no more to ride a bus or a Tube at the end of his four year term than they did at the start.

Meanwhile, he kept on wooing London's business, striving to bestride the mainstream and consign Goldsmith to the margins. On the evening of Brown's cross-examination Khan addressed a gathering of members of London First at the office of big league commercial property and real estate advisers CBRE. He performed with confidence and seemed well received. Heads nodded as he pledged to review the workings of the London Enterprise Panel, a partnership body chaired by the London Mayor. It is a formal example of mayors' "soft power" capacity to convene, galvanise and persuade. When Khan assured his audience that "I don't create the jobs or the growth or increase productivity" but could do his bit through Skills for Londoners towards creating a favourable environment for it, he was pushing at an open door.

There were, though, a couple of jarring moments. An economist from a major engineering firm observed that London might be unique in having no public transport on Christmas Day. Were there not compelling economic and social reasons for changing that? A senior consultant with Savills, another major provider of property services, asked for reassurance that a fares freeze wouldn't result in a fall in transport investment with unwanted knock-on effects for house-building. Might Khan not have to put up taxes to compensate?

Khan answered the second question first. "The research Savills does is really good," he began: "I wish you'd read some of it." The ripple of laughter was slightly nervous, before Khan explained that his tax-raising powers were strictly limited and set out his stall for making "good, but flabby" TfL more efficient. To the economist's question, he replied that he'd done "about 3,000 hustings" over the past months and no one had brought up running buses and Tubes on Christmas Day before. This got a big laugh, but it was a serious inquiry. Khan, sensing the need for it, rowed back from his initial flippancy: yes, he recognised that Christmas could be a lonely time for many, especially if they couldn't get around; he would come back with a serious answer.

Afterwards, Khan discreetly sought reassurance from a sympathiser in the audience that he'd done well and expressed exasperation that his fares plans were being questioned. "Mike Brown himself has told me my figures add up," he said, and it was a matter of record that Khan and Brown had met at the Labour conference. He need not, perhaps, have worried about how London First felt about him. He had a head start over Goldsmith simply by being willing to turn up. It was murmured that the Tory was proving difficult to pin down. It seemed he wished to focus his energies elsewhere.

*****

A starting point for understanding the political geography of Greater London is to split the metropolis into its Inner and Outer areas. Broadly speaking, Inner London is strong for the Labour Party while Outer London favours the Conservatives. Boris Johnson's victories in 2008 and, by a smaller margin, in 2012 had been attributed to a "doughnut strategy" of mobilising Outer London voters who've long tended to be older, more affluent and more guarded about change than their Inner Londoner counterparts. There are more of them, too – nearly five million out of the then total Greater London official total of 8.2 million according to the 2011 census, which, in line with Office for National Statistics practice, categorised 19 of the 32 London boroughs as Outer. Also, they are more likely to vote.

However, Outer London is very far from homogenous. There are even different ways of defining it: the ONS excludes the boroughs of Newham and Haringey from it but includes Greenwich, while the 1963 Local Government Act, which created the boroughs, does the reverse. Outer London boroughs range from the prosperous, genteel Richmond in the south-west, where Goldsmith has his parliamentary seat, to working class Barking and Dagenham, once home to a famous Ford motor car factory and still home to an old East End diaspora. So even Johnson's winning "doughnut" wasn't blue all the way through and demographic change was turning it redder.

The census data revealed that over the previous ten years, some Outer London areas had become populated by larger percentages of Londoners from ethnic minority groups and also marked by higher rates of poverty. A broad-brush portrait shows the proportion of Outer Londoners who are white projected to fall to little over half by 2021 compared with 74% in 2001. The percentages of people owning their homes were falling, while those of people renting privately were on the up. Around 60% of Londoners officially defined as being in poverty now inhabit Outer London for a range of reasons including the effects of the recession and benefit cuts, incomers settling in the cheaper suburbs because Inner London has become too expensive, and some outward displacement for the same reason.

These trends looked to have helped Labour in recent elections. Four of the five boroughs the party gained control of in 2014 were in Outer London: Merton, Croydon, Harrow, where it re-established its grip after a group of Labour councillors had broken away, and most notably Redbridge, which Labour had never run before. It also came very close to gaining the Conservative stronghold of Barnet, while in suburban Ealing and Hounslow it greatly strengthened its grip. The general election too had indicated that Labour was gathering strength outside its heartlands: five of the seven seats it gained were in Outer London: Ilford North; Enfield North; Brent Central; Ealing Central and Acton; Brentford and Isleworth.

But none of this meant the patisserie metaphor was stale. Goldsmith's strategists firmly believed the doughnut could still nourish a Conservative campaign. The Tory had been warning residents of Hornchurch, a town near the border with Essex 15 miles from London's centre point of Charing Cross, that Khan's fares freeze would ruin its high street. They'd been active in neighbouring Romford, another town within the borough of Havering, whose council includes seven Ukip members and had already voted to leave the European Union. Goldsmith's commitment to the doughnut was also in keeping with his claims to care about local communities and smaller firms. Outlying London has cultures, histories and concerns to which Tories often relate and Labour in the past had often failed to hear. Goldsmith wanted them to know he was listening.

But Khan had his big ears on too. His was "a 32-borough strategy," he said. Below dark skies in glum rain he joined canvassers one Saturday afternoon in the armpit of the north circular and A12 major roads near Ilford. Even an escaped party balloon racing across the sky was grey.

Ilford is the largest town in Redbridge in the north-east of Outer London. A quarter of it is forest and parkland and three-quarters of its homes are owner-occupied. Yet the census found a population rising towards 300,000 compared with 240,000 in 2001 and 57.5% of its residents to be from ethnic minorities, up from 36.5% ten years earlier. Londoners of Indian, Pakistani and Bangladeshi descent form the largest of these groups, in that order. "The upwardly-mobile Tower Hamlets crew," Khan remarked: "That's the London story: you do well and you move out, just like Jewish Londoners did in the past."

On the knocker, Labour spirits were high. But in one front porch came a low. A woman, white, well into middle age, came to the door. Might she cast a vote for Khan? Alas, no. "I don't think a Muslim can represent Christians," she explained. Maybe the old doughnut still contained plenty of blue jam.

*****

Another part of London's voting population illuminates by its very existence both the extraordinary cosmopolitanism of the city and the rights it confers on its residents. According to official figures over 500,000 of the capital's current population of 8.6 million and rising are citizens of European nations other than Britain and yet entitled to vote for London's mayor. Just over 2.2 million Londoners had voted in the 2012 mayoral election. The potential for non-British Europeans living in the British capital to influence the 2016 result was therefore obvious.

The EU referendum date had been fixed for 23 June, just seven weeks after the mayoral vote. A poll conducted in January had found 55% of Londoners wanting to stay in the EU compared with 45% who wanted to leave. Khan sensed an opportunity.

In Redbridge, he joked that he'd be ready to campaign alongside Goldsmith to keep London in Europe. The joke, of course, was barbed, as the Tory's Euroscepticism was well known. The following day, Goldsmith announced that he would indeed be backing the campaign for a British exit – a "Brexit" as it was known. His decision was overshadowed, first by Boris Johnson announcing that he would be doing the same and then by Cameron questioning Johnson's motives. Cameron had already announced that he would step down as Prime Minister before the next general election. Johnson was many people's favourite to succeed him as leader of the Conservatives and the country. "I am not standing for re-election," Cameron told the Commons: "I have no other agenda other than what is best for our country." This thinly veiled rebuke entertained the media for several days.

Then Khan moved to isolate Goldsmith on the issue; to further depict him as a fringe politician, out of touch with mainstream London opinion, including that of London's bigger businesses. An interview on BBC Newsnight gave him his most public opportunity yet to declare his willingness to "join a Conservative Prime Minister to argue for staying in the European Union". He claimed that a Brexit could end up forcing non-British EU citizens to exit London.

Where did Goldsmith's EU stance leave his campaign? Would it consign him to the political periphery, show him to be out of step with even his own party leader as Khan hoped? Or might it be profitably stirred in to a cocktail of anger, anxiety and dislike of immigration that could mobilise that critical mass of Outer London voters on whom his hopes of winning depended?

Six

March

The town of Sevenoaks in Kent is not as lampooned as a wellspring of Little England attitudes as its neighbour Tunbridge Wells, but its reputation is similar. The MP for Sevenoaks since 1997 has been Conservative Michael Fallon. In 2009, Fallon become caught up in a scandal surrounding expenses reclaimed by MPs. The Daily Telegraph reported that between 2002 and 2004 he had overcharged the public purse in relation to a flat he'd bought in Westminster to the tune of £8,300.

"Mr Fallon regularly claimed £1,255 per month in capital repayments and interest rather than the £700-£800 for the interest component alone," the paper said. Fallon said it was a mistake, for which he accepted responsibility. He repaid part of the money to which he had not been entitled and was allowed to offset the remainder against other expenses relating to the flat for which he had not previously claimed, such as legal fees and utility bills.

Fallon had paid £243,000 for the flat. In 2005, he reclaimed £499 he'd spend on a television for it, plus £69.50 for a digibox. In 2006, he claimed £126 for repairs to the flat's boiler, £170 for repairs to tiles in its bathroom, £282 for electrical repairs and £225 for carpet cleaning. In December 2006, he sold the flat for £295,000, making a profit of £52,000, and reclaimed legal fees of £1,774,50.

He then bought another flat in Westminster for £728,000 and reclaimed £1,500 for the cost of new curtains, nearly £1,000 for a freezer and laundry white goods and £1,795 for a bed, although the bed claim was reportedly later reduced to £1,000. The interest on the mortgage for Fallon's new flat was around £2,100 a month – almost three times as much as on his old flat. He reclaimed it. The Telegraph added that Fallon also owned what it described as mortgage-free "large house" in Sevenoaks, which is less than 30 miles from Westminster.

At the time of these disclosures, Fallon was a member of the Treasury select committee, which keeps an eye on the expenditure and administration of Her Majesty's Treasury, Her Majesty's Revenue and Customs and the Bank of England. Earlier in the year he had been critical of the excesses of the banking industry. Three years later, apparently without irony, David Cameron made him his minister for business and enterprise. By July 2014 he had promoted him to Secretary of State for Defence. In April 2015, the month before the general election of that year, Fallon wrote an article for the Times accusing Ed Miliband of stabbing his brother David in the back in order to become Labour leader and of being willing to do the same to the United Kingdom. It was regarded by connoisseurs of Lynton Crosby's methods as an example of his "dead cat" tactic: feeding compliant media outlets a lurid "story" about your opponent by way of a stooge to distract attention from your own candidate's shortcomings.

In early February 2016 Fallon attended an arms trade banquet whose organisers thanked him for his "tremendous support". Near the end of that month Cameron announced that with the help of his government a British arms company had done a deal to sell fighter planes to Saudi Arabia, a nation with some of the most oppressive Islamic laws in the world, where 70 people were beheaded in the first two months of 2016 alone following sometimes secret trials and on the strength of evidence often extracted under torture.

On the last day of the same month Fallon made a speech in support of Zac Goldsmith to fellow Conservatives in Kentish Outer London Bromley. Fallon described Sadiq Khan as a "Labour lackey who speaks alongside extremists" and as "unfit" for the role of protecting Londoners. The following day, 1 March, the Evening Standard reported Fallon's remarks on its front page. The Daily Mail followed up. So did the Daily Telegraph. So did the Sun. In all this media coverage, Michael Fallon's enthusiasm for selling weapons to an Islamic state that tortures and beheads was never mentioned.

*****

On 5 March, the Mail on Sunday reported that what it called a "key aide" and "speechwriter" to Khan had posted a series of nasty comments on Twitter. Most of these had appeared in 2012 and 2013, before the young man concerned had been taken on as an apprentice at Khan's parliamentary office. The observations of Shueb Salar had amounted to a social media compendium of gutter hate slang, jeers and sneers. Poor white people were "chavs", gay people were "faggots", women were "bitches" and "hoes". Bengalis smelt bad. He'd made jokes about rape, the murder of girlfriends and the proper place for women being in the home. In May 2013, the day after off duty soldier Lee Rigby had been hacked to death in Woolwich by two deranged Islamists, Salar aired the conspiracy theory that the atrocity "was probably fake".

It was plain that a younger Salar had made an intimate connection with his inner creep. Khan's team suspended him immediately. The following day, when images emerged of him posing with a gun at a shooting range with accompanying witticisms about being a hitman, he resigned. How did Salar get under Khan's wing? A composite profile from sources close to the Labour candidate suggested a young man with a difficult history who had, as the Mail reported, been an amateur boxer and secured a law degree from the University of Bedfordshire. Boxing and law: two things he had in common with Khan. The Mail said Salar had "toned down the content of his tweets" after starting work as an assistant to Khan at his Commons office in November 2014, a role that mostly involved dealing with constituency casework. According to Khan's campaign he was never a "key aide" or a "speechwriter" for the Tooting MP. Now he was out of a job.

You can take the boy out of the street and maybe, with the support of a Labour politician eager to help one with brains and ambition become a better human being, you can take the street out of the boy. But unless you take the street out of his Twitter archive he can be transformed into an electoral liability by dirt-diggers trawling for every possible way to insinuate to voters that the Labour politician in question secretly tolerates things he says he deplores.

*****

As Khan's team tried to hose down these media fires, Goldsmith paid a visit to the Richmond branch of McDonalds. Staff showed him how to construct a Big Mac. Goldsmith told the Richmond and Twickenham Times that he had "absolutely loved the experience" and described the burger he had inspected as "a very tempting little object". He praised the ethics of the fast food franchise: "I think they have moved forward in an environmental sense more than any company I can think of." Two days later he visited another branch in Sidcup, most of which is in the borough of Bexley, another Tory Outer London stronghold. Boris Johnson went with him. He was photographed holding a glossy document named "Khan's £1.9 Billion Experiment." It asked: "Who will he tax? What will he cut?"

During this time Khan attended a fundraising night in his honour held at the Royal Vauxhall Tavern, one of the capital's most celebrated gay venues. When defending having "shared platforms" with Suliman Gani, the Muslim cleric who had starred in February's glut of "extremist links" stories, he had said that Gani had taken a dim view of Khan's support in parliament for equal marriage rights for same-sex couples. It turned out that Gani had been an imam at the Tooting Islamic Centre and therefore active in Khan's back yard. Khan also made it known that his backing for gay marriage had resulted in a disapproving fatwa, a judgment of Islamic law, being issued against him.

The contrast between the London Khan inhabited and the one familiar to Goldsmith was further sharpened by an interview the

Conservative gave to GQ magazine. He said he no longer had time for playing poker and talked about a smokeless cigarette he had discovered – a "heat stick" which helped him meet his continuing nicotine needs. He revealed that he was wearing one of his late father's suits and that the label read "Savile Row bespoke". Goldsmith explained that he mostly wears just two or three suits or "a jacket and some dark corduroys". The two men had already published their tax returns. Goldsmith's showed that since becoming an MP in 2010 his total income from his trust fun and sale of assets had topped £10m. Khan's earnings since he'd become an MP in 2005, five years earlier than Goldsmith, had totalled £647,000. Nearly all of this had been his wages as an MP and a government minister. There was an extra £3,250 from TV and radio work, of which £1,500 had been his fee for appearing on the BBC's satirical Have I Got News For You. Khan's campaign said he'd donated this to a charity.

Goldsmith opened a new line of attack on Khan. In an article for the Daily Telegraph he praised "our magnificent green belt, stretching from Oaks Park in Sutton to Stanmore Common in Harrow to Thames Chase in Havering". He called this a precious resource, which "encompasses forests, meadows and walkways that have been treasured by generations of Londoners". But now danger lurked among the hedgerows: "Today, London's green space is under threat." That threat, he warned, took the form of the "Corbyn-Khan experiment" which would include "paving over our parks".

Goldsmith's evidence for this claim rewarded close inspection. He wrote that Khan "has said that if he wins the green belt will be up for review, admitting in a recent interview that 'building on the green belt would be something we could look into'". The interview Goldsmith referred to had appeared in the Economist in early February, conducted by the magazine's pseudonymous columnist Bagehot. The passage in which the London green belt was discussed went as follows:

> **Bagehot**: You've said in the past that the green belt is "sacred." But quite a lot of the [London] green belt is golf courses and high-intensity farmland. And the evidence suggests that it means Londoners have to be crammed ever more closely together within it. Are you sure it's the right approach to put the green belt on a pedestal in that way?

> **Khan**: I am committed to protecting the green belt. New homes can be built on brownfield and there is plenty of scope to fix the housing crisis without building on the green belt...so my point is: you don't need to go to the green belt if you use land already available in London properly...People who advocate most for building on the green

belt are developers. What happens is, as night follows day, the price of those pieces of land will go through the roof if the mayor says, "let's build on the green belt." They are crucial as the lungs of our city. If I was persuaded that all the possible pieces of land in London were being used sensibly and were built upon, building on the green belt would be something we could look into. But we are nowhere, nowhere, nowhere near there.

Goldsmith, or whoever had drafted the Telegraph article for him, had not misquoted Khan. He had, though, completely misrepresented what Khan had said to his interviewer. By selecting one part of one sentence from Khan's Economist interview, the Goldsmith article told Telegraph readers that Khan's intentions for the green belt were the precise opposite of what Khan had actually told the Economist they were.

Goldsmith's other evidence was that in 2009 when he was a government minister Khan had "approved plans to rip up parts of our green belt to make way for development". What Goldsmith did not mention was that the green belt land in question was not in London but elsewhere in south-east England. It was not, therefore, part of "our green belt" at all as far as Londoners were concerned. The move had been part of the Brown government's plan to meet housing demand. Had he not lost the election, around 6,000 new homes might have been constructed in Oxfordshire and Surrey.

But this attack was not primarily about facts. It was not even about the green belt. It was about symbolism and anxiety. The menacing idea of "our" green and pleasant land being "concreted over" has long been employed as a mobilising metaphor for keeping the dark and alien of the inner city at bay. Goldsmith's strategists' heads and his own countryman's heart seemed to well understand the power supposed threats to the green belt can exert in those parts of the metropolis that don't think of themselves as being part of London at all.

Goldsmith's depiction of green belt land itself was as misleading as his quote from Khan's Economist interview. Less than a quarter of it is open to the public or enjoys special environmental protections. Nearly 60% of it is used for intensive farming, the sort of thing Goldsmith deplored when he edited the Ecologist. About 7% is taken up with golf courses. In other words, most of the green belt in London is inaccessible to Londoners and isn't very green.

The previous week, housing charity Shelter and planning consultants Quod had published a joint report on London's housing supply with the self-explanatory title When Brownfield Isn't Enough. It argued that if housing supply in the capital was to be doubled to around 50,000 new homes a year it would be necessary for the next mayor to ask boroughs with green belt land in their territory to work with him to make some of it available for new homes.

This was not the first expert analysis to urge such a step: think tank Centre for Cities, London First and London School of Economics professor Paul Cheshire had all done the same. Cheshire had calculated that no less than 1.6 million homes could be built at average density levels on just a fraction of the roughly 125 square miles of green belt turf Greater London contains.

The day after Goldsmith's article appeared, he, Khan, Siân Berry and Caroline Pidgeon formed the panel for a hustings held by environmentalist think tank the Green Alliance at One Wimpole Street in Central London. All four ruled out any erosion of the green belt in Greater London. Three days after that, the Institute for Public Policy Research published the 120-page report of its London Housing Commission.

This drew on the knowledge of the cream of the capital's housing experts and was chaired by Lord Bob Kerslake, former head of the UK civil service, the Department for Communities and Local Government and the government's Homes and Communities Agency. In line with the Shelter and Quod report it urged the next mayor and boroughs to immediately review the status of green belt land close to public transport sites as part of increasing housing supply in London to the 50,000 a year required. But although both Goldsmith and Khan had pledged to up house building to that level, neither of them was going to commit to touching green belt land.

*****

While all this was going on, polling firm Opinium was contacting just over 1,000 Londoners for the first survey of mayoral voting intentions since YouGov's in early January. Survey responses were gathered online between 2 March, which was the day after Michael Fallon's "Labour lackey" speech was reported, and 7 March, which was the day Shueb Salar resigned. In other words, the research period coincided precisely with the slew of bad news stories about Khan.

The results were published in the Evening Standard on 8 March. They showed that 31% of respondents said they would vote for Khan with their first preference vote compared with 26% who'd vote for Goldsmith. This was a 2% smaller lead than Khan had enjoyed from January's YouGov poll but a solid one nonetheless. Answers to a separate question about second preferences made still more encouraging reading for the Labour man. Just over half of the survey sample expressed one, of which 31% favoured Khan and only 16% Goldsmith.

This gave Khan a 55% to 45% advantage over Goldsmith once second preference votes were taken into account - exactly the same lead that had emerged from YouGov's "head-to-head" question, which was another way of measuring the effect of second preference votes. If a true reflection of voting intentions, the Opinium poll meant that even during the height of negative media coverage Khan had lost little if any ground to Goldsmith since the Conservative had woken up at the start of the year. He was ahead with all age groups except the over 55s. He was even slightly ahead among Outer Londoners - and way ahead with Inner Londoners.

Respondents were also asked if they agreed with Goldsmith's charge that Khan was "radical and divisive". This question found agreement with 29% of them while 27% disagreed – a small difference, within the 3% margin of error pollsters acknowledge. They were also asked to agree or disagree with the Khan team's counter blast that Goldsmith had been indulging in "coded racism". In this case, there was a much wider split: 34% agreed and only 25% did not.

Khan also emerged well from questions about how much he and Goldsmith were trusted on the nine policy areas those surveyed had said mattered to them most. Khan outscored Goldsmith on reducing crime, on public transport fares and reliability, on dealing with transport unions and on tackling unemployment. He was even slightly ahead on environmental issues. On airport expansion they were neck and neck - perhaps Goldsmith's credibility had suffered due to his prediction in November on LBC that he "couldn't be more confident" that a third runway at Heathrow would be ruled out by the end of the year. The one category where Goldsmith led was in "attracting business and investment".

This data, taken at face value, pointed to only one conclusion: that Goldsmith's campaign was going nowhere, in part because one third of London voters thought it disagreeable. The poll was discouraging for the smaller parties too: Peter Whittle, Siân Berry and Caroline Pidgeon each secured only 2% of first preferences and George Galloway trailed with less than 1%.

There were, though, crumbs of comfort for Goldsmith. One was the continuing high proportion of voters – around a quarter of them – who had yet to make up their minds. The other was the potential for Outer London to rally round him. Goldsmith was only just beginning to try to exploit this. If the Opinium poll indicated that his campaign was struggling, it could also be seen as evidence that its best bet was to carry on in much the same way. And there was one further crumb: the possibility that the polls were wrong.

*****

On the night the Opinium poll was published, a
gala fund-raising dinner was held for Khan at
the London Sea Life Aquarium. The compere
was Margaret Hodge, the Labour MP for Barking
and a highly experienced politician. Hodge had
considered seeking to become the mayoral
candidate herself, but in the end had decided to
back Khan. Her endorsement had carried weight,
not only because she was a former leader of
Islington Council and government minister but
also because of more recent high profile exploits.
In 2010, Hodge, who was born in Cairo in 1944
to Jewish refugee parents, had retained her
parliamentary seat of Barking by hammering Nick
Griffin, leader of the neo-Nazi British National
Party, into a distant third place. She had then won
praise for her combative chairing of the House of
Commons public accounts committee, responsible
for overseeing how government departments
spend their money. The main guest speaker of the
evening was another senior Labour figure: Jeremy
Corbyn.

The aquarium is in the County Hall building that
stands right across the Thames from the Houses
of Parliament. It had previously been home to the
Greater London Council and before that the London
County Council, these being the two London-

wide administrative bodies that had preceded the Greater London Authority and the mayoral system. A vexed Margaret Thatcher had abolished the GLC in 1986. Her ire had been inspired by Ken Livingstone's activities which had included hanging banners showing the number of British people unemployed and, in July 1983, greeting Sinn Fein president Gerry Adams in London following his election as MP for Belfast West the previous month. The move caused widespread outrage. Adams's visit was at the invitation of Livingstone and Corbyn, himself newly elected to his Islington North seat.

Corbyn's words to the aquarium diners harked back to that period of London government when Livingstone's GLC and a number of Labour boroughs had declared their opposition to Thatcherism and adopted bold stances on an array of social issues, opposing racism, supporting gay rights, promoting equality for women. These boroughs had included Hodge's Islington. For Corbyn, the cultural pluralism of London owed much to such initiatives and he expressed his confidence that a Labour Mayor Khan would help sustain them. He said nothing about Khan's declared enthusiasm for billionaires. He said nothing about Khan's criticisms of him and John McDonnell. There was solid applause.

Khan spoke later. He thanked Corbyn, made some seafood jokes, referred in passing to the tedium of being trolled by George Galloway, and assured everyone, in case they hadn't already heard, that, yes, he intended to be the most business friendly mayor ever. The mutual politeness across a policy divide, with Hodge serving as a kind of Islingtonian diplomatic bridge, could have been read as sincere or strained or simply a practical expression of the barge pole relationship being beneficial to both, if at times a bit uncomfortably.

The most significant thing was the simple fact of Corbyn's attendance. His and Khan's Living Wage outing to Arsenal remained their only public appearance together and Khan wanted it that way. His campaign and Corbyn's office had stayed in touch. Relations were mostly cordial, sometimes a little tense. Khan's autonomy was always maintained.

Straight after he'd become the mayoral candidate, core members of his team, which included Jack Stenner along with experienced Labour spin doctor Patrick Hennessy, campaign chief David Bellamy, policy director Nick Bowes and senior advisers Leah Kreitzman and Alison Picton had, as one of them put it, locked themselves in a room and vowed to fight their campaign their own way. They'd figured that Khan's backstory and personality would outshine Goldsmith's. They'd set about relentlessly exploiting this. Though determined to be essentially positive in their approach they adopted one dictum from Lynton

Crosby's. "Getting the barnacles off the boat," was his expression for refining policy messages for maximum simplicity and efficiency. The following morning bore this out resoundingly.

*****

One Canada Square is the tallest building in Canary Wharf, the newer of the capital's two powerhouse business districts. It is the second tallest in London after the Shard. Four fifths of the way up is Level 39, the whole of which is devoted to companies involved in financial technology innovation. It offers widescreen views down a long curve of the Thames to where the City of London, Canary Wharf's ancient yet permanently rejuvenating rival, makes its own imposing mark on the skyline. This panorama formed the backdrop for the launch of Khan's full manifesto. The emotional message was unmissable: the little guy from Tooting can rise to bestride the big city of his birth.

Tessa Jowell introduced him. This was a coup for the Khan cause. A journalist who knows Jowell and had bumped into her in the vast foyer downstairs had sensed that she was feeling fragile. But Jowell mounted the podium with a brave and generous smile. Khan's campaign, she said, should be "a love song to London". She spoke with a catch in her voice.

Khan spoke with greater command than he had from a smaller stage in a humbler setting in Isleworth a few weeks earlier. "London is the greatest city in the world," he said: "But we're at a crossroads." Journalists rolled their eyes – they'd heard that one before. This was not going to deter candidate Khan. Again calling up the language of opportunity, he portrayed the city that formed the backdrop to his words as a mighty enabler and framed the mayoral task as helping it to perform that function better.

The headline pitch of A Manifesto For All Londoners was adjacent to the One London gospel Jowell had preached, identifying common ground between workers, environmentalists, communities and cutting edge capitalists in desiring "a more prosperous, safer and greener future for our city". Business, prosperity and opportunity were linked together in the first section of the document itself. "Our manifesto will remove the barriers to competitiveness, productivity and growth," Khan said. But also: "I will call on our great companies to help make London a beacon of fairness and opportunity once again," seeking their help with building homes and developing skills.

It was 9 March. The previous day had been International Women's Day. Khan said he would be "a proud feminist in City Hall," addressing the gender pay gap by publishing the mayor's "first ever annual pay audit and requiring large contractors to do the same". He promised to protect green spaces, prioritise clean buses and establish Energy for Londoners, a non-profit company to nurture low carbon energy. To would-be first time house buyers he pledged more shared-ownership options, and, to renters, his new, local income-linked London Living Rent tenure, his mayoral lettings agency and more pressure on bad landlords.

Through all of this ran a broad streak of interventionist energy, a hands-on, can-do attitude that Khan wished to personify and hoped would connect and enthuse. He contrasted his approach with Goldsmith's, which he characterised as having "no vision for the future and no plans to fulfil Londoners' potential - just a negative campaign to distract Londoners from my opponent's lack of experience, substance or values". He drew attention to the Conservative's Brexit stance: "The EU referendum will take place just six weeks after the mayoral election. It will define the future of our city." To close, he said he was confident that London would choose his "positive vision and a real plan – a vision for a city in which opportunity is restored, the potential of innovators and entrepreneurs unleashed and the sky's the limit for optimism".

It was a speech to match the setting – elevated, ambitious and touched with the emotion of hopes and dreams. Some of that made the transition into media coverage. But Khan's fares arithmetic continued to come under scrutiny. ITV London's

Simon Harris grilled him on the numbers, concluding that he wouldn't come up with a clear figure for the policy's cost. And in a huddle with print journalists Khan was pressured to respond to figures provided by a distinguished independent academic who had produced an estimate of £800m-£900m. If correct, Khan's calculation of £452m was sounder than the £1.9bn Goldsmith was touting, but it was still a lot wrong.

Khan responded that his efficiency measures would, in any case, "bring in way above £800m". He suggested that a further look at Transport for London's recent business plans would reveal a limited relationship between its figures and reality. There was no doubt in his mind that they played "creative finances" in order to protect their budgets. His interrogator put it to him that his figure was based on a different measure of inflation from that used by TfL: the consumer price index rather than the retail price index, which always generates a higher figure. But Khan insisted that his sums were solid and, for the first time on the record, said they'd been endorsed at the very top of TfL.

"What I'm saying is, even Mike Brown – even Mike Brown – accepts that by merging the engineering departments of Tube and surface [transport modes] you can save, in his words, hundreds of millions of pounds. Number two, in relation to consultancies and temporary staff, even Mike Brown accepts that they can cut that by a huge amount. They accept that if they reduce that they can save hundreds of millions of pounds per annum. They also accept that TfL could have a commercial arm that does what it should be doing, bringing in revenue streams of significant values. They accept they could be doing much, much better. They also accept, by the way, that if they use the land they own sensibly, they could bring in hundreds of millions of pounds. So even if we accept your figure of £800m-900m, we'll get there, and some."

Khan also had something to say when asked about the Goldsmith campaign's strategy: "It shows how desperate they are that they're doing this sort of stuff." He called Michael Fallon "a proxy" for Goldsmith who, in allowing the Defence Secretary to be deployed in the way he was, betrayed fundamental failings as a candidate: "You receive advice and you either accept advice or you reject it, right? My point about being inexperienced and lacking vision is that he hasn't got the experience to say to TfL, 'You've got to be on the side of Londoners'. It also means you've got to stand up to those advising you. If you want a clean, positive campaign fizzing with ideas, you say to those wanting to play desperate politics, 'No, I don't want to do that.' He should be stronger."

*****

The following evening, Khan was back in Canary Wharf, this time at the offices of accountancy giant KPMG for a hustings with Goldsmith, Caroline Pidgeon and a stand-in for Siân Berry, who was absent for family reasons. It was organised by the London Business Forum, an umbrella organisation for the capital's different business groups – the umbrellas' umbrella, so to speak. The setting was plush, the audience smart. The exchanges were rather nostalgic.

The contrasts in pitch and policy between the two frontrunners were reminiscent of the mid-1990s, when Britain's two biggest political parties wrestled for the prize of exuding superior economic competence. Goldsmith again portrayed himself as a protector, in this case of London's resilient super-growth, which he again suggested Boris Johnson deserved credit for.

Much else from Goldsmith was familiar: the greater stress on middle income home ownership, the "common sense" – something Tories often seem to believe they have a monopoly on – that Khan's fares freeze would prevent new transport infrastructure from blazing a house building trail. Goldsmith also proposed making "superfast broadband our fourth utility", devolving funds to businesses and councils to help match skills training with jobs, and writing a requirement for low cost commercial space into his planning policies. "Affordable office space is every bit as important as affordable housing," he said.

Here was a Goldsmith not much sighted since an ITV Late Debate in early February, hosted by Simon Harris, where he'd got the better of Khan. Goldsmith had been cool, fluent, measured and persuasive. Khan had seemed agitated by comparison. But both candidates had bullshitted freely. Khan had made a poor job of rebutting the £1.9bn fares freeze cost claim. Goldsmith had contrasted himself flatteringly with the Labour man, dubbing him "a principal architect" of national Labour's transformation into what he called a "snarling anti-business monster" under Corbyn.

This last point by Goldsmith was somewhat at odds with history. Gordon Brown, who'd made Khan a minister, had been the leader of Labour's "prawn cocktail offensive" when Tony Blair was steering the party towards its 1997 general election landslide win. Khan was now offering a similar pro-active partnership, with his fares promise as part of that – businesses were among those bothered by high transport costs. He underlined his promise to create "a new business advisory board of experts – not political allies". He was eager to talk about the EU. Goldsmith was not. "It's an opinion, not a policy," he said. Khan also mentioned being a Muslim – and that "Zac and his mates" kept mentioning it too.

*****

The contrast between Khan's wish to embody a harmony of capitalist endeavour and worker prosperity and Goldsmith's appeal to suburban unease became still more explicit when the latter released his first detailed policy document. Where Khan had produced a single booklet addressing all policy areas, the Conservative followed the precedent of previous mayoral campaigns by giving each policy theme a separate small volume. The first of these was his Living Environment Manifesto, which was set out under four headings. Significantly, the first word of the first of these was "protecting".

There are tensions within the ideologies of all political parties. Conservatism's greatest strains are between the urge to accumulate and the impulse to preserve. Goldsmith's old concerns about Devonshire cheese-makers and the gluttony of global capital may have made him more receptive to the side of that debate that seeks safeguards against forces for change felt to be threatening. Certainly, he judged it helpful to his mayoral bid to depict Khan as a potential agent of such change.

The Foreword to his document mischaracterised the green belt as being substantially "centuries old" and the idea of building on it as "a huge temptation to experiment with short term fixes" – a view directly contrary those reached by an array of planning and housing experts of various political leanings. It repeated the questionable claims Goldsmith had made in the Daily Telegraph about Khan before pledging to tighten the rules about the green belt in the London Plan.

As Goldsmith wrote, these stated that "the strongest protection" should be given to green belt land and that development on it "should be refused except in very special circumstances." For Goldsmith, this allowed too much wriggle room: "As Mayor, I will issue new planning guidance making it unambiguously clear that protected means protected." He did not, however, mention that the caveat allowing some small green belt erosion was there because of Boris Johnson, whose London Plan it was. And, as at the Chamber of Commerce hustings at the LSE, neither did he reprise what he'd said at the Institute of Directors back in September: that in the event of continuing population growth it might be necessary to discuss developing green belt land in 15 or 20 years' time.

Goldsmith levelled charges against the record of Ken Livingstone instead. Under him, Goldsmith wrote, "London lost the equivalent of at least 900 football pitches of green belt". The size of football pitches varies, but 900 would cover roughly 2.5 square miles. If Goldsmith's figures were sound, the loss of green belt during the eight years of

Livingstone's mayoralties had therefore been miniscule.

Like Khan – and unlike all those housing and planning experts – Goldsmith insisted that brownfield sites for housing were so plentiful that building on protected sites need not even be contemplated. To emphasise his point he said that Crossrail 2, a planned new north-east to south-west cross-London rail link, could "unlock the development of 200,000 new homes". The problem here was that a report from the Lord Adonis-chaired National Infrastructure Commission, drawing on Transport for London research, said the building of 200,000 new homes could not be facilitated without "the limited release" of green belt land near Crossrail 2 stations. Unearthing this inconsistency at the website City Metric, Jonn Elledge described Goldsmith's claims about Crossrail 2 and protecting the green belt as disingenuous – and Khan's too, on the same grounds.

Many of Goldsmith's other "living environment" pledges looked very similar to Khan's: both men vowed to support "sustainable" energy production including solar power through a mayoral energy department; both pledged more recycling, biodiversity and enclaves of verdant tranquillity. The difference was that these messages were directed at different people. Khan's were built in to a "progressive" pro-growth message; Goldsmith's were integral to an appeal to suburban resistance.

*****

Mid-month brought more opinion poll cheer for Khan. A new YouGov survey found that he had the same seven-point first preference lead over Goldsmith as he'd enjoyed in the same firm's January poll. When undecided respondents were stripped out, the margin widened to nine points. Whittle was a distant third on 5%, followed in close order by Pidgeon and Berry. Galloway's YouGov rating had halved to just 1%.

However, YouGov's commentary on its figures pointed out that although "don't knows" had fallen from 30% to 23% since the start of the year, they remained numerous. The company's national map of Eurosceptic sentiment showed some potential for the Brexit-backing Goldsmith to exploit, with Havering and Bromley topping the list of London boroughs that way inclined. Another detail of the poll, measuring likelihood of voting, suggested that support for Khan might be softer than that for the Conservative. The lie of the land was still hard to gauge with confidence. Were there still movements beneath the surface that could yet undermine the Labour man?

The "extremist links" theme surfaced again when Babar Ahmad gave a couple of interviews. Born and raised in Tooting, Ahmad had been no ordinary prisoner when Khan had been to visit him in jail. A fighter with fellow Muslims in Bosnia during in the mid-1990s collapse of Yugoslavia, he'd returned home and run a website which carried coverage of conflict zones involving Muslims from round the world. Two articles published on the site offered support to the Taliban regime then in charge of Afghanistan. In 2003, Ahmad was arrested by British police in London and then locked up for eight years without charges being brought while the US government sought to have him delivered across the Atlantic to stand trail in a US court.

His case became a cause celebre for those opposed to the UK-US extradition treaty. Politicians of all mainstream parties expressed concern. Campaigners demanded he be tried in the UK or not at all. In 2009 Ahmad was awarded £60,000 in damages after the Met admitted that its officers had subjected him to "serious, gratuitous, prolonged, unjustified violence" and "religious abuse" when arresting him. Ahmad was eventually flown to the US in 2012. Two years later in Connecticut Ahmad admitted two charges of "conspiracy and providing material support to terrorism" as part of a plea bargain. His American judge said she did not believe he was a supporter or plotter of terrorism. Ahmad was soon released and returned to Britain in July 2015.

Speaking publicly for the first time since his return to the UK, Ahmad was asked about his relationship with Khan. He said they'd known each other as children and that Khan was "probably an acquaintance more than a friend". Khan had visited Ahmad in prison twice in his early days as an MP, a status that provides protections against covert surveillance. A 2008 report into the matter for the then Labour Justice Secretary documented those two visits, which took place in May 2005 and June 2006, and an earlier one Khan made in October 2004, ten days before he ceased to be a practising solicitor.

The report said that, although the October 2004 meeting was defined as "a legal visit", it did not appear that Khan had ever been instructed by Ahmad to act as his solicitor. In January 2015, four months before becoming an MP, Khan applied to become an "approved visitor" to Ahmad. This category of visitor excludes MPs. According to the report, Khan described Ahmad as "a friend whom he had known since they were 12 or 13 years old; they were locals and attended the same mosque". The report then said that in March 2015 Khan was "added to the list of Babar Ahmad's approved visitors as a friend entitled to make open visits".

Being an approved visitor made him liable to monitoring when he visiting Ahmad. As the report explained, such approval was no longer needed by Khan after he became an MP. But the report also said that Khan had not applied to be re-categorised after winning his Commons seat and "nor did he inform the prison authorities that he had become a Member of Parliament". It found that a small number of prison or police officers involved knew Khan had become an MP by the time of his visits to Ahmad in May 2005 and June 2006, but "had no reason to regard this as significant". The report concluded that the monitoring of the conversations between Khan and Ahmad on those days "was carried out lawfully under the legislation".

That was the key content of the report at the time. Eight years later it was Khan's categorisation as a "friend" of Ahmad in his approved visitor application and what exactly that word meant about Khan's relationship with him that formed the core of a discussion on the BBC's Daily Politics programme. For a representative of the Henry Jackson Society, a British foreign policy think tank named after a famous anti-Communist US politician, it raised grave questions of national security: "We need to understand exactly what the relationship was," he said.

*****

Meanwhile, the Goldsmith campaign team was busy stuffing envelopes. They contained letters signed by the Prime Minister. They contained leaflets. The messages each sent were carefully tailored according to whom their intended recipients were. Among those who were sent versions of the letters and leaflets were members of some of London's South Asian communities.

One version of the leaflet was designed for the capital's 70,000 Tamils, among whom the most common religious practice is a form of Hinduism. Under the heading "Sadiq Khan won't stand up for London's Tamil community" the leaflet claimed that when Khan was a government minister "he did not use his position to speak about Sri Lanka or the concerns of the Tamil community in parliament". This was a reference to a period when London saw a major demonstration about the plight of Sri Lankan Tamils towards the end of that country's long and bloody civil war. Beneath that line on the leaflet came the following about Khan:

> "His party SUPPORTS A WEALTH TAX on family jewellery"

Exactly the same point about family jewellery was made on the Goldsmith leaflet aimed at the 600,000 Indian Londoners, as were claims that Khan was in thrall to union bosses and that he'd make voters pay for an "experiment" he planned for the transport network. The difference was the foreign policy component, which, unlike the Tamil leaflet, made reference to Jeremy Corbyn. It said that Khan "supported" Corbyn who "wanted to BAN [India's] prime minister Modi from visiting the UK". It added, meaningfully, that Khan did not attend the vast welcome event held at Wembley stadium for Modi when he visited London in 2015.

Considerable craft went into these messages. The accusation in the Tamil leaflet about Khan not speaking about Sri Lanka when he was a minister neglected to mention that his position had not been in the Foreign Office. It was, therefore, not his job to speak about Sri Lanka publicly. Had he done so it would have gone down badly with colleagues whose territory he'd have casually invaded. The absence of any mention of Corbyn may have been because Tamils in London and elsewhere hold him in high esteem thanks to his consistent support for them over human rights abuses down the years.

By contrast, the attempt to link Khan with Corbyn in the "Indian community" leaflet by means of Modi was very pronounced. It was also rather disingenuous. Modi had already been banned from entering Britain following outbreaks of violence across the state of Gujarat between Muslims and Hindus in 2002. He had been Gujarat's chief minister at the time and was accused of siding with fellow Hindus during the riots, in which more than a thousand people died. Modi was also banned from entering some other European countries and the US. The UK ban lasted for ten years before being lifted in 2012. When the British government began making overtures to Modi the following year, Corbyn asked for the ban to be reinstated. However, as Labour leader he had dropped the demand before meeting Modi during his London visit.

As for Khan, he had attended the Downing Street reception held for Modi during his visit to London and, according to his team, also received "a bit of advice" from Modi's communications chief during the Labour candidate selection contest. It was, though, the "wealth tax" allegation in the leaflets that prompted most remark. To substantiate it, the Goldsmith campaign cited John McDonnell making a case for what he'd called "a fairer taxation system" and others called a "wealth tax". It was pointed out that jewellery is included in taxable assets in India and also in France. Voters were therefore invited to infer that Khan was in favour of a tax on family jewellery that as mayor he would have no power to impose and that the man who was at least four years from even standing a chance of becoming Britain's Chancellor hadn't actually said he wished to raise.

But public critics of the "jewellery tax" attack were more annoyed by what they alleged it revealed about Conservative attitudes, contending that it was rooted in a patronising stereotype. Gold and other jewellery do enjoy a special significance in some aspects of Hindu family cultures but did Tories think hoarding heirlooms was an all-consuming preoccupation? Uma Kumaran, who had narrowly failed to win the parliamentary seat of Harrow East for Labour in the general election said it showed that Conservatives believed that Hindu Indian and Tamil Asian voters "are primarily concerned with their family gold and small businesses" and judged it "ill-advised".

Some was also ill-directed. Londoners of Indian birth or descent include a significant minority of Sikhs. Soon, Sikh media were reporting that "thousands" of items of Goldsmith's "Indian community" literature had been sent to the addresses of Sikh Londoners and observing that this seemed based on the assumption that "all the 120,000 [London] Sikhs were middle-class Hindus, running family businesses".

There was, in fact, Sikh-themed Goldsmith material sent out as well. Leaflets for them, which also addressed "London's Punjabi community", led with the "wealth tax on family jewellery" line. A letter signed by Cameron tried to push a foreign policy button. It said that Goldsmith had campaigned for Sikhism's holiest place of worship, the Golden Temple in the Punjabi city of Amritsar, to "remain in the hands of the Sikh community". Recipient Anita Singh, the arts and entertainment editor of the Daily Telegraph, took to Twitter to describe the leaflet as "despicable negative campaigning" and the letter as "patronising crap" and to observe that "Goldsmith weirdly thinks everyone called Singh is sitting on a stash of gold".

Then came a Telegraph article by Councillor Binita Mehta, leader of the Conservative group on

Watford Council. She expressed her sincere hope that Goldsmith would become mayor but took issue with the way he had approached her fellow British Indians in London:

> "We must always be sensible and sensitive. Not all British Indians are fans of Modi – I have my reservations – nor do we particularly care about the current prime minister of the country our grandparents are from. Most of us care much more about bread and butter political issues: housing, tax and the NHS, just like other citizens of other ethnicities."

She argued that "in pursuing the suburban Indian vote" such a "blanket approach can seem stereotypical and patronising and will certainly put people off". She described bumping into the Goldsmith campaign's chairman Nick de Bois - the former MP for Enfield North since losing the seat to Labour in 2015 – on an Underground train and sharing with him her anxieties about "our clumsy approach". According to Mehta, de Bois "admitted that we should have seen this coming and acted sooner to avoid embarrassment".

How widely such sentiments were shared was impossible to quantify. The Goldsmith camp said the "jewellery tax" line was an attempt to humanise a campaign message. And it wasn't only presumed

Tamils, Indians and Sikhs who got letters from the Prime Minister. One recipient of a more bog standard missive singing Goldsmith's praises fitted none of those descriptions: a Mr Kenneth Livingstone of Cricklewood.

*****

The London Mayor does not control the day-to-day work of the police – their operational functioning – but is ultimately responsible to voters for their performance. Khan knew that Goldsmith's campaign would do all it could to suggest he was unfit for the task. Already, Goldsmith had taken credit for George Osborne making no further cuts to the Met's finances in his spring budget. Five days after that, on 21 March, Khan went to One Great George Street, a Grade II-listed Edwardian conference centre just off Parliament Square, to make a speech about London's security.

He arrived heavily armed: accompanying him as he walked into a handsome reception room heavy with history and chandeliers was Jacqui Smith, who had been Home Secretary under Gordon Brown. Smith said she was delighted to introduce Khan and declared: "I trust him to keep London safe." She reminded their audience of supporters and journalists that she and Khan had worked together in government. "He's a serious and experienced politician and a passionate Londoner," Smith said: "And I'm impressed by the way that he's turning his personal and political experience into a plan to tackle extremism, radicalisation and crime." Khan had shown "considerable personal bravery and grit in the face of undeserved personal slurs and personal threats," she went on: "He knows what it's like for him and his family to have been targeted by the extremists because of his mainstream British views."

Smith handed over to Khan. "Londoners face a deadly threat from extremism, radicalisation and terrorism," he said: "I will be the British Muslim who takes the fight to the extremists." With those words, Khan did something other than provide an assurance about fanatics, cops and bombs. He took a step towards the most hostile prejudices ranged against him and looked them in the eye. It was a move to construct the best possible defence from a position of potentially great weakness. It was a rational gambit, but it required a certain nerve.

Khan talked about 7/7: "I remember desperately trying to contact my wife to check that she and our daughters were OK." He called extremism "a cancer that is eating away at our society" and "a problem that is getting worse". Neither the government nor the wider society were doing enough to challenge it, he claimed: "A growing number of people in London are being indoctrinated and radicalised into a perverse and disgusting ideology."

He said he welcomed plans to increase the Met's armed response capacity, but that it was vital to be sure London could cope with a Paris-style attack: "On day one of my mayoralty, I will order a full and comprehensive review of London's emergency services' capability to deal with a major terrorist incident." Armed officers could be assured of his backing. But he would work on prevention too: "I will ensure that people from different communities meet and engage with one another."

Again, he urged "mainstream British Muslim voices to speak out loudly and clearly" against "a poisonous ideology". Then, for the third time in his speech he declared: "I will be the British Muslim who takes the fight to the extremists." It was the boldest personalisation of his campaign so far and perhaps the most necessary – the sternest part of the Muslim Test addressed head on.

After the speech Khan declined to match Goldsmith by ruling out any increase in mayoral council tax. He reckoned to keep that option open in case police budgets were cut again. "How can a serious mayoral candidate promise to freeze council tax over the next four years?" he demanded: "It shows a lack of experience, a lack of judgment and someone who's taking a risk with public safety."

He again offered his credentials as a warrior against extremism, rather than an indulger of it: "I'm the person who when he first stood for parliament had people outside the mosque that I've prayed in all my life saying that I was somehow an apostate and I would go to hell. I'm the person who when he voted for same sex marriage had a fatwa against me and had to speak to my daughters about the importance of being safe." He also had a message for Sikh, Tamil and Indian Londoners: "Your gold is safe with me."

Seven

April

There comes a seductive stage in many election races when a consensus starts to form that one side cannot win and the other is on the home straight to victory. Early signs of this started to appear. Two more opinion polls set the scene. A new Opinium survey gave Khan an increased lead as a first preference choice and a 54% to 46% win in the second round run-off. The following day, new figures from ComRes found that 44% of those saying they were "likely" to vote made Khan their first preference for mayor while only 37% went for Goldsmith. Khan was up 2% from the same company's previous poll, conducted in March, and Goldsmith was down by the same amount. The run-off split gave Khan a 10% advantage. If those figures spoke the truth, Goldsmith was getting nowhere except perhaps further behind.

Well-connected heads popped above Pundit Parapet: at the Telegraph, James Kirkup, anticipating a Khan win, called Goldsmith's campaign "underwhelming" and "openly negative" adding that "even London Tories privately admit" that it was "faltering". The Spectator's Isabel Hardman reported "those around" Goldsmith being "in despair" and that Tooting Tories were already preparing to fight the parliamentary by-election that would be held once a Mayor Khan stepped down as local MP. The headline of her piece said: "Zac's campaign is as good as over."

Along with these discouraging signs came some embarrassments for Goldsmith. The Spectator published what it called his "record of failure" in business, listing a string of failed ventures going back more than ten years. He then had an unhappy experience in the back of a London black taxi. The capital's cab drivers are famous for having to master the Knowledge, a unique and extensive memory test of the city's streets and places of interest. The BBC put both Goldsmith and Khan through their own mini-quiz whilst riding in the back of a black cab. Chief political correspondent Norman Smith doubled as cabbie and inquisitor.

Khan's first question was about the row over the regulation of Uber, the app-led private taxi hire phenomenon that was undercutting London's traditional licensed trade and threatening its future. Khan was for imposing higher standards on Uber drivers, including a language test: "Basic English should be a requirement if you're a public servant." Then he was asked if he believes in God. No hesitation: "Yes." Was he offended by page three of the Sun with its topless female models?

"I'm not personally offended," said Khan but "as a feminist and a dad" he thought it wasn't great. Would he consider taking in a Syrian refugee? Khan hedged. He said he'd have to talk to his wife about it. With two teenage daughters, it might be difficult. But, ok, yes.

This last was one of those questions, like being asked to promise to end rough sleeping, that politicians cannot answer no to without risking unwanted attention from campaigners and press. Khan was more definite when pressed on one of his signature slogans – being "the most pro-business mayor ever". Smith put it to him that his record didn't make him seem very pro-business. He had, for example, voted against cuts to corporation tax.

But Khan spotted an opening: he was the only candidate who'd helped run a successful business, his former legal practice; he would jump on a plane with George Osborne and fly around the world on trade missions if it helped London; he'd campaign with the Prime Minister to stay in the EU. Smith asked him how he thought that kind of talk went down with Jeremy Corbyn, from whom Khan had continued to keep his distance – a brief canvassing encounter in Islington was all they had added to their list of joint public appearances since donning their Gunners scarves back in November.

"I'm not Jeremy Corbyn's representative to London," Khan said. Did he regret nominating Corbyn for the Labour leadership contest? He didn't. Did he think Corbyn as leader put Labour in a better position to win a general election? Khan answered a different question. He said it would have been wrong to deprive party members of the chance to vote for him. Smith said: "It sounds like you're a supporter of his." Khan said: "Of course I'm a supporter of the Labour Party." Asked if he was a bit of a flip-flopper, Khan said he was against the strain of Labour thought that disliked compromise with the electorate: "I'm a democrat, I'm a pluralist, I want to win elections."

Then came the questions that really mattered – the pratfall section of the interview. Smith asked Khan to name the stop on the Northern Line that follows Charing Cross when heading south. "The Embankment," said Khan. Correct. Which London football club played at Selhurst Park? "Crystal Palace," said Khan. Correct. Khan stumbled when asked to name London's oldest museum – it is the British Museum – but he was able to say he'd worked in an office in close-by Museum Street when he was a lawyer and he came up trumps on a question about EastEnders, the long-running BBC soap. Khan knew that the first barmaid of the Queen Vic pub was called Angie. She was married to a wrong-un, nicknamed Dirty Den. Khan told Smith that as a youth he'd had a paper round: "I used to deliver to Dirty Den's mistress! True story!" Khan's fare was £22.40. "Thank you mate, ta-ta," he said as he hopped out of the cab close to his home, the South London Artful Dodger arriving back in his manor.

Goldsmith's cabbie quiz was broadcast the next day. Smith asked him if it difficult for him, a very wealthy man, to vote for cuts to welfare benefits received by people who are dirt poor? In mid-March, Goldsmith had been dropped as a patron of a Richmond disability charity after voting in favour of a £30 cut in financial support for disabled people. "I've stood on a manifesto at both elections which involved reforming the benefit system to make it pay to work," Goldsmith replied. Did he believe in God? "I have a great reverence for the natural world," Goldsmith said: "There is a magic in the world. But I'm not religious in a conventional sense." Was he offended by page three of the Sun? "No. I'm not offended by page three. It's not something I would promote. But it's not something I'd want to ban."

Next, Uber and the future of black cabs. "I'm a huge fan of black cabs and I think it's essential that we ensure the black cab has a bright future," Goldsmith said: "You don't do that by banning Uber. I don't think you can ban Uber. It should be a requirement that Uber drivers and private hire vehicle drivers should have a basic grasp of London's geography." A "basic understanding of English," would be good too. There was also, in his view, an issue with the number of Uber drivers: "We think it may be becoming a congestion problem."

Then came the hard part.

"Who plays at Loftus Road?"

"I don't know. What's the answer?"

It was Queens Park Rangers. Next, which Central Line station came after Tottenham Court Road, heading east?

"I'm going to stop you there," said Goldsmith. He digressed: "Most people have a route or two routes, and they become like an extension of the body..."

The answer was Holborn. Goldsmith did know who the first landlord at the Queen Vic had been. But he did not know where the Museum of London is, despite having been there recently. It turned out he'd been to Loftus Road recently too.

Goldsmith was lampooned in the left wing media for his cab quiz failings, especially for his lack of football knowledge. What did the posh boy know of ordinary life? Three days later, BBC Radio London held a hustings. Khan, Pidgeon, Whittle and Berry were all there. For reasons that were not revealed, Goldsmith chose not to attend.

*****

The following day, Saturday 9 April, Conservatives gathered in Central London for their annual Spring Forum event. An all-star line-up was headed by David Cameron, Boris Johnson and Home Secretary

Theresa May, with Goldsmith in support. May and Johnson spoke about the mayoral race. That is to say, they spoke about Sadiq Khan.

May said she was worried when she saw Khan "in contortions" over Babar Ahmad and "when I see that he has shared a platform with a group backed by an extremist imam". Her conclusion was grave: "This is not the judgment London needs in a mayor at a time when we face a significant threat from terrorism." Johnson said: "Khan has shared platforms – to put it at its mildest – with some pretty dodgy people with some pretty repellent views."

Goldsmith spoke directly after Johnson. He praised him effusively: "It is a privilege to be following Boris Johnson on to this stage today. He is a formidable campaigner, a force of nature, and he has been a superb Mayor of London."

As he spoke, Goldsmith indicated Johnson, who was sitting just below him at the front of the audience. After re-running his standard script about his background – the colourful family history, the early, fearless crusading for right against wrong – he went through his action plan, including the mayor's responsibility for policing.

"I will keep our city safe," he pledged: "With the threats we face today at an all time high that is an awesome responsibility." He said he'd "protect" neighbourhood policing and officer numbers and put extra police on the Tube. "But most of all," he stressed, "I'll back the brave men and women who put their lives on the line so regularly in order to keep us safe".

Now, he too talked about Khan: "London cannot afford to have a mayor who opposed stop and search, whose party leader thinks there's a problem with shooting terrorists in our streets, a mayor whose career before becoming an MP involved coaching people in how to sue our police. On this issue there can be no ambiguity, there can be no looking both ways."

He then got on to boasting about his record as an MP, but was distracted in mid-flow. "Someone's phone is ringing here," he said, looking down at his lectern: "Shall I answer it?"

It became apparent that the caller's name was showing on the phone.

"It's Evgeny," Goldsmith announced.

He glanced down at Johnson again.

"Oh, it's *your* phone."

Goldsmith already had the phone in his hand and was heading Johnson's way.

"Here we are. Sorry. I shouldn't have said that. Here you are, Boris."

As he climbed back on to the stage, a blush crossed Goldsmith's face.

"I'll pause for a few moments," he bantered as Johnson dealt with the call.

There was only one Evgeny it was likely to have come from – Evgeny Lebedev, super-rich son of the super-rich Russian businessman Alexander Lebedev and owner of the Evening Standard. Johnson, from the floor, bantered back. It wasn't perfectly audible, but sounded like: "He's backing you. It's alright."

"Wonderful," said Goldsmith, recovering himself: "That is a huge relief. Thank you."

*****

On the morning of Tuesday 12 April, Goldsmith held a campaign rally at a community hall in Southfields, near Wimbledon. It followed a Sunday of further "extremist links" newspaper stories and, on the Monday, Khan tweeting Goldsmith directly: "Hey, @ZacGoldsmith. There's no need to keep pointing at me & shouting 'he's a Muslim'. I put it on my own leaflets." The words were accompanied by an image of a flyer saying Khan promised to be "The British Muslim who'll take on the extremists".

Proceedings in Southfields were behind schedule, heightening expectations that the phenomenon known as "Boris" would be taking a break from his Brexiting to appear at Goldsmith's side. Outside, a bespoke Goldsmith minivan proclaimed from its side panels that the candidate's policies would secure over 500,000 more jobs. This was the headline theme of the event. Its main effect, however, was to intensify the drumbeat denigration of Khan.

Johnson was already in the thick of this. The previous day he had devoted his regular Monday column in the Telegraph to repeating and elaborating on attack lines devised by Goldsmith's propagandists. He'd begun by reporting three tweets by a then Labour councillor in Luton, praising Adolf Hitler. Though acknowledging that the young woman in question had since "been removed" from the party, Johnson contended that her remarks suggested to him "that there is a cancer in Jeremy Corbyn's Labour Party".

He then documented other recent, well-publicised examples of aggressive anti-Israel views expressed by Labour Party members and argued that "to understand this anti-Semitic sickness" you had to recognise that "the Corbynistas believe in the most extreme ideology that Labour has ever espoused," and that there was a real danger that these "Corbynistas" would "capture the London mayoralty". Khan was included in Johnson's definition of a "Corbynista" because he'd nominated Corbyn for the leadership contest.

Then came the familiar "sharing platforms" list, including "jihadi flag-waving events sponsored by the Islam Channel, which has been criticised by Ofcom for condoning marital rape". Johnson did not mention the good luck message he'd sent to the same Islam Channel-sponsored event a few years later. But he did accuse Khan of "pandering to the extremists". Goldsmith, by contrast, he described as "a man of principle" who "must win".

This salvo had a political context other than the mayoral race: the vicious battle for control of the Conservative Party and Johnson's long-standing desire to lead it. The determination of some of his fellow Tories to prevent that ever happening could be detected in assessments of Johnson published by fellow journalists and erstwhile colleagues with Tory sympathies.

Soon after Johnson announced he'd be campaigning to leave the EU, former Conservative MP Matthew Parris had used his regular space in the Times to launch a scathing attack on him, describing "a pattern to Boris's life" marked by "casual dishonesty", "cruelty" and "betrayal" and accused him of being "sly" and having "a careless disregard for the truth".

It wasn't the first time Johnson had been savaged in this way. One of his former Daily Telegraph editors, Max Hastings, had denounced him as "a far more ruthless and, frankly, nastier figure than the public appreciates". Back in 2008, a few days before Johnson became mayor, his then fellow star of the Telegraph opinion pages Simon Heffer had accused him of a "blinding lack of attention to detail" and of a "ruthless ambition" selfishly pursued on the back of others' efforts. More recently, Heffer had characterised Johnson as "so self-serving that he cannot be relied on to put any other consideration first".

The Southfield activists awaited the arrival of this shining star. He turned up 20 minutes late, hunched, dishevelled, vaguely toad-like and seeming to emit an obscure private glee, as if revelling in having dragged himself away from something pleasurably furtive in order to make a grand display of decency. The activists rose as one.

"I genuinely think that a spectre is stalking London," Johnson began. He harked back to the Livingstone administrations, bemoaning their raising the congestion charge, something Johnson himself had done twice, and permitting the construction of high-rise apartment blocks, which Johnson had been allowing in ever-increasing numbers.

His audience guffawed. Johnson asked them if they wanted the next mayor to bring congestion charging to Outer London, something Khan had not proposed but which Johnson's own transport strategy acknowledged there might be a need for. They most certainly did not. Johnson told them that only Goldsmith could repel the Labour spectre. Again, he pronounced him "a man of principle".

Goldsmith began by genuflecting to the "Boris" god. He then made a neat joke: "I want to tell you a little bit about myself. I am the son of a grocer..." The audience got it. "Well, technically," conceded Goldsmith, winningly: "My father sold a lot of

Marmite and Bovril." He then ran through his action plan. But the bite of the speech came near the end when he spoke about the police: "Most of all, I will back our brave men and women as they put their lives on the line for London."

This wasn't to be a pledge about beat bobbies or beating burglary. Goldsmith was invoking mortal peril. He was summoning the spirit of righteous war: "I will be the mayor who is on the side of the heroes who protect and who keep our city safe. My rival will be the mayor whose career involves coaching people in how to sue our police; a man who's given platforms and oxygen, even cover, to people, over and over and over again, who seek to do our police and our city harm; a man who has tried to silence questions about those events by shamelessly accusing anyone who raises those questions of Islamophobia. There can be no ambiguity at all, no looking both ways when it comes to keeping Londoners safe."

The "extremist links" charge sheet was now made dramatically more serious. To questions about judgment and insinuations of lurking sympathises was added the accusation that Khan had actually aided and abetted violent jihadists. He had "given platforms and oxygen" to such people; he had provided them with "cover". The implication was that the election of a Mayor Khan would somehow enable terrorists to go about their business more easily. Goldsmith's audience warmly approved.

Following his speech, Goldsmith joined journalists in a side room. He was asked about the letters and leaflets sent to Tamils, Sikhs and Indians. Did he think these had helped or hindered his campaign? Why had tailored material been sent to those three groups of people in particular? Why not the South Koreans of New Malden or the Latin Americans of Southwark? Why not to Muslim Londoners as a group? Why not Bengali Londoners or Pakistani Londoners, these especially in view of his praise for his former brother-in-law Imran Khan?

"I have sought to reach out to all and I've used every tool available to do that," Goldsmith replied. "And it's not true to say that I have not reached out to the Pakistani, the British Pakistani..."

But not with targeted, tailored leaflets...

"With leaflets outside mosques and with mosque visits and public meetings and with all kinds of events," he went on: "The reality in a campaign of this sort is that time is short – we've only got 23 days left. I've got to use every second of every minute to talk to as many people as I possibly can, and that's everyone. There's no no-go area in London, there are no boroughs I'm not doing meetings in, there are no communities I'm not trying [to talk to]."

It was true that Goldsmith had visited mosques during his campaign, and on that very day he had tweeted good wishes to Bengali Londoners, the great majority Muslim, who were celebrating Pohela Boishakh, the Bengali New Year. But why were those three categories of people - Indian, Sikh and Tamil Londoners - given such dedicated attention, including letters from the Prime Minister?

"But that's not true," he began. "I have sought to...the means don't exist to scientifically reach every single person in London".

Could more light be shed on this lack of scientific means? Not by Goldsmith: "My job is to use every tool available to reach out to as many people in London as possible and that's what I've done."

His next question came from a different reporter. It was blunt: "Are you a racist?" Goldsmith said the question was "absurd." OK. Did he, though, understand why some might see his "ethnic targeting" as "creating or intensifying ethnic divisions?".

"I can understand why Sadiq Khan's team might want people to think that," Goldsmith replied: "But the reality is the opposite." He insisted that Khan's past attendance at events where people who do hold extreme views have spoken gave grounds for questioning his judgment: "To pretend otherwise is, I think, deeply irresponsible."

Asked about other Tories who had attended or endorsed the very same events he'd criticised Khan for attending, Goldsmith said he didn't know about them. He denied that it was hard to square the claim that Labour planned a jewellery tax on non-Muslim South Asian Londoners with his insistence that his campaign had been positive. He said its "overwhelming thrust" had been about his action plan and that this had been "a thread that's run through every single piece of literature that's gone out". In response to a question from the Evening Standard's City Hall editor Pippa Crerar, he took full responsibility for this material: "Every piece of literature that comes out of my campaign is literature that I've read and seen. Of course."

That morning, Yvette Cooper, a former shadow home secretary, had written an article for the Times. She had described Goldsmith's attacks on Khan as starting as a "subtle dog-whistle" and "becoming a full blown racist scream". She'd accused Michael Fallon, Theresa May and Boris Johnson of the campaigning equivalent of "pointing and shouting 'Don't vote for him, he's a Muslim,'" and of deterring anyone from an ethnic minority from seeking public office.

"Well," Goldsmith said: "The implication is that a majority of Muslims share platforms, give oxygen and even excuses for people with extreme views, who preach hate. And that is not true. The overwhelming majority of British Muslims do not give platforms to people with extreme views, do not provide excuses for them, do not provide cover for them. Just to be clear I am not suggesting, and nor have I ever suggested, that Sadiq Khan has extremist views. That's not the point. This is an issue of judgment. I think it's legitimate for newspapers, for me, and for anyone else with an interest in the outcome of this race, to ask those questions."

It was pointed out to him by Crerar that the betting markets were saying that Khan had an 88% chance of winning. Had the Conservatives given up in London? Goldsmith answered a slightly different question: "The support I'm getting is as much as the party is physically able to provide."

Was he really passionate about winning?

"You don't get involved in a campaign of this sort without wanting to win," Goldsmith replied: "It's a serious undertaking. I have a sort of double role now, I think, to protect London against what would be a catastrophic error."

Someone else asked if he regretted the way the campaign was turning out. Goldsmith said: "I've sought to keep the campaign as positive as possible and I will continue to do so for the next three and a half weeks."

*****

That evening Goldsmith returned to the Institute of Directors headquarters in Pall Mall, scene of the Tory candidate selection hustings in September. This time he was there to debate Khan at the invitation of the Square Mile newspaper City AM. This time, the mood was less friendly.

The pair entered the hall by a side door to a soundtrack of London Calling by The Clash – possibly a first for the IoD. Khan made his opening pitch. "London is the greatest city in the world," he began: "But we are at a crossroads." To some in the building, this assertion came as no surprise. Khan played his opportunity cards: from council house to successful business career to a tilt at the mayoralty. He set out his housing and transport stall. He would be "a mayor for all Londoners". He said: "I'll be the most pro-business mayor London has ever had." This would include taking "a lead from the front" to remain in the EU.

So far, so familiar. No barnacles in sight. But there was an extra sail on the mast. "I've been disappointed at the tone of the campaign run on behalf of my opponent," Khan said: "It's been negative. It's been divisive. I'll continue to be an advocate of the best of London – a mayor who will unite the city, not divide it."

Goldsmith towered at his side. Journalists in the house included national commentators and broadcasters, a sign that the mayoral race was now attracting media interest beyond the London specialists. "I'm here to talk tonight about how my action plan for London will benefit London's businesses," Goldsmith began: "But before I do that I hope you'll forgive me for addressing what I think is a really important point."

The characteristic courtesy foreshowed an all-out assault: "In recent days, Sadiq Khan and his supporters have accused my campaign of being Islamophobic." Goldsmith addressed his words to Khan directly: "Sadiq, I have never referred to you by your religion. That has never happened. To suggest otherwise is wrong and it is offensive. Faith is irrelevant to anyone's ability to do this job. But there are serious questions about you and your judgment."

If this was a spontaneous departure from his script, Goldsmith was well prepared for it. He had a list: "Your letter to the Guardian in the wake of 7/7, blaming terrorism on British government policy. Your choice to defend – your *choice* – to defend a self-confessed 9/11 terrorist, your choice to take on the British government to overturn a ban on the US hate preacher Louis Farrakhan, your step-by-step legal guide on how to sue the Metropolitan Police, your decision to share a platform with an extremist who called for Jews to be drowned in the ocean and who threatened fire throughout the world, dismissing this preacher's words as mere 'flowery language'."

He went on: "These are some, just some, of the decisions you have made. These are facts, not smears, and it is right that you are being scrutinised because you are standing to be Mayor of London, the greatest city in the world. You shout 'Islamophobia' to close those questions down, but this is nothing to do with Islam. Nor is anyone suggesting, Sadiq, that you have extreme views. This is very simply about your judgment."

Khan was not going to be drawn into the point-by-point rebuttal he might have offered to Goldsmith's charge sheet. This could have included saying that he'd never actually met the Frenchman Zacarias Moussaoui, who eventually pleaded guilty to a conspiracy charge related to the 9/11 terrorist attacks on the US, when he was brought in as a consultant for the defence team under an arrangement made by the British government in the context of opposition to the UK-US extradition treaty. It could have entailed his saying that he'd known nothing of or about the man Goldsmith said had called for Jews to be drowned at the time he was alleged to have said them (as indeed he later would). It might have included Khan arguing that it is no bad thing in a democracy for citizens who believe they've been mistreated by police officers to know how to seek redress.

All this might have made for an absorbing debate. But it would not have been in Khan's interests to have it. Instead, he played his fatwa-and-death-threats defence and went on to say there was a good reason for Goldsmith's "talking about me and issues that are both negative and divisive. It is because this man has no vision for this city. And it disappoints me to say it, because he is a good man. Before Lynton Crosby's team took over his campaign, he had exciting ideas. He was fizzing with ideas. They are being drowned by this negative, divisive campaign".

Goldsmith replied that it wasn't only him who had concerns about Khan. Did he think the press were "engaging in Islamophobia when asking about those platforms you shared, defending people with the most extraordinary, abhorrent views?"

Khan didn't answer. He said instead that the debate should be about policies: "I'm the person, by the way, whose campaign has Muslims, Jews, Christians, Sikhs, Buddhists, those who are of no organised faith, rich, poor, old, young, gay, lesbian." He called on his comic timing: "We even have people from Yorkshire supporting my campaign."

Later, Conor Sullivan, London correspondent of the Financial Times, asked for more elucidation about Babar Ahmad. Why did Goldsmith and the Home Secretary think Khan's support for Ahmad disqualified him from being mayor? What was Khan's response to Goldsmith's case? Goldsmith reeled off a history of Ahmad's exploits, describing him as having created "an online facility designed to help recruit people engaged with the Taliban" which was "a fund-raising vehicle as well". He said Ahmad had "pleaded guilty to having engaged in indirect, secondary terrorist activity". He said that

Ahmad was "supported throughout that time," by Khan, in the first place as a friend and then as an MP.

Khan then tried to turn the tables. He said he was "amazed by the selective amnesia of Zac Goldsmith," and that Goldsmith had campaigned to stop Ahmad's extradition to the US, just as he had. Goldsmith responded sharply: "It's just complete and utter nonsense that." He accepted that he'd been "a critic of our extradition arrangements," adding that he had campaigned on the issue on behalf of constituents and others. But: "To suggest that means I was campaigning on behalf of Babar Ahmad when I'd never even heard of him until quite recently is an extraordinary thing to say."

Khan had the last word: "There are very good journalists here and they'll do their homework."

*****

The following morning at just after 8:00, Adam Bienkov demonstrated that such homework had been done. He published film footage from YouTube of Goldsmith speaking at a meeting of anti-extradition campaigners held in the House of Commons in 2012. In it, Goldsmith told his audience that Ahmad was one of many people who had been "chewed up" by what he called "our lopsided extradition arrangements". He said:

218

"Babar Ahmad's is a story that has caught peoples' imagination. I have been bombarded with letters from my local constituents. I've lost track of how many. I've had so many letters [about it]."

By then, Goldsmith had given an interview to the Evening Standard, which was carried prominently. He had again accused Khan of poor judgment and of "giving platform, oxygen and cover" to extremists. Goldsmiths said he had decided to speak out only after Khan's tweet about "pointing at me and shouting 'He's a Muslim.'" He accused Khan of "hiding behind Britain's Muslims" and said it was "obscene" that he should behave in such a "totally shameless" way. He also cited a particular individual he thought Khan had spent too much time with: "To share a platform nine times with Suliman Gani, one of the most repellent figures in this country, you don't do it by accident."

Gani is a Londoner. He saw the Evening Standard and was displeased. His unflattering mention in the Sunday Times in February had not been the last he'd received during the mayoral campaign as a result of his connections with Khan. These went back more than ten years and largely arose from his being a fellow resident of Tooting. Gani had even been the imam at the Tooting Islamic Centre until 2013. Being called "repellent" by Goldsmith drove him to retaliate on Twitter.

First, he posted a photo of himself and Goldsmith standing together in a London street.

Of itself, this was not necessarily significant: well-known politicians are often asked to pose for photographs with people they don't know and will never meet again. But Gani offered clarification. It seemed his encounter with Goldsmith occurred because they had attended the same politics-related meeting: "I was no stranger to Zac. I attended the "be a Councillor" event by invitation & introduced myself to Zac before the photo was taken."

Gani had other photos for the world to enjoy. One showed him sharing quite a small and intimate platform with Jane Ellison, the Conservative MP for Tooting's neighbour constituency of Battersea. In another, he posed with Tania Mathias, Tory MP for the south-west London seat of Twickenham. Gani wrote that Mathias had been seeking his help with making contact with a mosque in Hounslow. "Is that repellent?" he asked, rhetorically. Most revealing off all was a snapshot of Gani with a man called Dan Watkins. Watkins had been the Conservative candidate and principal challenger to Khan in the Tooting seat at the general election. "I supported Dan in 2015 general elections," Gani wrote and inquired: "If repellent, why @Conservatives wanted my support then @ZacGoldsmith." @ZacGoldsmith did not get back to him.

*****

Within two days of Goldsmith's "giving cover" speech in Southfields and the City AM debate, his past sympathy for Babar Ahmad and the backing his party's parliamentary candidate in Tooting had received from the "repellent" Gani had been quite widely reported and the revelations were doing good business on social media. A wider audience was also learning that Gani and Jane Ellison, along with other Conservative MPs, had made common cause in the campaign to have British citizen and Londoner Shaker Aamer released from the controversial US detention camp Guantanamo Bay on the south-eastern coast of Cuba. By the end of Thursday 14 April it seemed unlikely that any journalist paying close attention to the mayoral race or any campaigner involved in it would have been unaware of Goldsmith's past support for Ahmad – whom he'd claimed to have heard of only recently – or Gani's for the Conservative Party.

Yet all this seemed to have passed the notice of Max Hastings when he filed a furious column for the Daily Mail of Monday 18 April. Addressing the race for City Hall, he was scathing about Goldsmith – "a rich kid with nice manners but no 'bottom'" – and said Boris Johnson, about whom he'd once been so rude, had been "terrific in the role" of mayor. But these were not Hastings's main concerns. He had convinced himself of the "desperate importance" of preventing a Khan victory. Khan's being a former chair of Liberty was brought to readers' attention. There was ominous mention of a "mask of moderation". And Hastings wrote that Khan had "spoken nine times at meetings addressed by the hard line imam Suliman Gani, who last year reportedly joined a campaign to establish an Islamic state".

This last suggestion stemmed from claims by the Conservatives that, at an event held in Bedford on the night of the Paris attacks, which Gani had spoken at, some speakers had called for British Muslims to struggle for such an entity – "an Islamic state" - to be formed in Britain. Though he had yet to utter a public word about the mayoral election campaign, Gani was becoming a significant factor in it. He was in the limelight again that evening when the BBC's Andrew Neil brought up Khan's alleged nine-time platform sharing past with him during a TV debate, which also involved Goldsmith, Whittle, Pidgeon and Berry. Gani's Tory connections didn't crop up then either. But their most glaring omission from the public discourse about him was yet to come.

On Wednesday 20 April, nearly a week after Gani's recent associations with various Conservatives had been reported by the Independent, the Spectator, the Guardian and others, none other than David Cameron failed to mention them when denouncing Gani as a way of denouncing Khan. And he went much, much further in his attack on the imam than anyone had before. During his weekly Prime

Minister's Questions appearance on Wednesday 20 April, Cameron put it to the House of Commons that Khan was unfit to be London Mayor because he had appeared on platforms with Gani who, in Cameron's exact words, "supports IS".

It was an extraordinarily serious charge. Cameron had described Gani as an enthusiast for Islamic State – not "an Islamic state" in the abstract, but the militant Islamist group whose various names include "Islamic State" – "IS" for short – which had been slaughtering its way through Iraq and Syria, had carried out the Paris attacks and was a big reason why UK security chiefs feared that a terror attack in London or elsewhere in the country was highly likely.

Cameron had damned Khan for associating with Gani. Yet it had been known for days that Gani was a man who had helped Cameron's own party in its unsuccessful attempt to end Khan's career as an MP.

Moreover, the claim that Gani was a supporter of IS – or ISIL or ISIS or Daesh - seemed contradicted by an image of a poster advertising an event called The Evils of Isis that had been circulating on social media. The venue for the event was the South London Islamic Centre and the scheduled date was 1 January 2016. Gani was listed as a speaker.

Cameron's words were met with crises of "racist" from Labour MPs opposite. Other uncomplimentary words might also have been used.

Could Britain's Prime Minister really have been unaware that, just a year ago, Gani had helped his own political party in its attempts to unseat Khan? Had word of this not reached him almost a week after the media had made it known to a wider public? Had his decision to use Gani for attacking Khan been made in ignorance of the complicating factors or had a cost-benefit analysis been made?

Gani accused Cameron of "defamation at its highest level" and had more to say about his connections with London Conservatives. In an interview with LBC Radio broadcast straight after PMQs, he told the station's political editor Theo Usherwood that he hadn't just turned up at the "be a councillor" event he had referred to on Twitter where he'd met Goldsmith. He said that, on the contrary, Dan Watkins had invited him to the gathering, which had been set up by an organisation called the Conservative Muslim Forum and held the previous autumn.

Furthermore, Gani said that when he'd raised a question at the meeting – and a photograph had by then emerged of Gani in attendance – Watkins had introduced him to the others present. This, in Gani's view, underlined that Watkins had already known him from the general election the previous spring. Gani added that he had even supplied Watkins with canvassers. He said, too, that he had "never promoted terrorism or violence" and that the allegation that he supported the Islamic State group appeared based on a misconstrued remark made by someone else at a meeting – presumably the Bedford one - where the historical context for the emergence of IS had been discussed.

Gani also vindicated Khan's previous claims that the two men had fallen out over Khan's support for same marriage. In Gani's view, this had shown Khan putting his political career before his adherence to Islam: "We were very disappointed when that took place...He is a Muslim himself and understands what marriage is about." For now, though, Gani's disappointment with the Tories was more intense. He believed they had used him "as a scapegoat to discredit Sadiq Khan".

*****

After PMQs, Goldsmith's team circulated a dossier of Khan's alleged "links" with fanatics down the years. Cameron's claims about Gani and Khan received the widespread attention he'd intended. Not all of it was deferential. Westminster political correspondents reported attempts by his official spokesperson to justify his claim that Gani "supports IS". She said that what the Prime Minister had meant was that Gani had "called for 'an Islamic state' at a meeting where he'd spoken, although no verification was forthcoming. She was pressed for clarification. Was "an Islamic state" in theory the same thing as the violent jihadist organisation Islamic State, in her view? "I think you can have a debate about what 'IS' means," came the reply.

There was, though, a much larger debate already underway about what Goldsmith was doing to try to damage Khan. The Prime Minister's intervention intensified it. The following day, experienced political columnist Peter Oborne, a resident of Chiswick and a lifelong Conservative voter, wrote that for the first time ever he would place his cross next to the name of a Labour candidate. Not only would he be voting for Khan, he would be doing so "proudly". He called Goldsmith's campaign "the most repulsive I have ever seen as a political reporter". In America, billionaire businessman Donald Trump was on his way to becoming the Republican Party's presidential candidate using bellicose anti-Muslim rhetoric. Oborne deemed Goldsmith's tactics "horribly reminiscent" of this.

The article attracted much attention, including from Khan who tweeted it enthusiastically to his followers. On the same day, 21 April, a new YouGov opinion poll appeared. Its fieldwork had been conducted between the 15 and 19 April – before PMQs, but closely following Goldsmith's "giving cover" speech. It found Khan to be enjoying his biggest lead yet – a massive 20 percentage points after second preferences were added in. The figures excluded "don't knows" and "would not votes" and were weighted according to respondents' likelihood to vote. Recalling the "radical and divisive" leaflet and the mailshots to non-Muslim South Asian Londoners, YouGov's commentary concluded: "The strategy seems to have backfired."

*****

That evening, Khan and Goldsmith locked horns once more, returning to the Royal Geographical Society for a debate jointly organised by Centre for London and the Evening Standard. The contrasts and the tensions between them now felt as stark as their policy wares and speeches were familiar. Goldsmith, giraffe-like next to his terrier opponent, spelled out his action plan once more, pledged to freeze council tax, to work well with the government, to keep his promises as mayor as he had as an MP and to protect, protect, protect: the transport budget, green spaces, Londoners themselves and "what Boris Johnson has achieved" would all be safeguarded from the dangerous Khan alternative.

Khan's address pinned his entire prospectus to his life story as a Londoner: the opportunities, the schools, the jobs, the London helping hand. "I'll be the council estate boy who fixes the housing crisis, the bus driver's son who makes commuting more affordable, the businessman who helps our business to grow and prosper and the British

Muslim who takes the fight to the extremists and does what's necessary to keep Londoners safe," he said. And there was more: "I want to unite our great city and bring all Londoners together to make London even better. That's the clear choice at this election. The choice between a united London and a divided one, between a One London approach with a mayor for all Londoners and a Donald Trump approach with a mayor for..."

His final words were drowned by laughter and applause. As the debate progressed, the "shared platform" and "extremist links" questions kept coming, including from the floor. Yet Khan's confidence was obvious, even from the back of the hall. At the end of the debate, Goldsmith loped quickly away from the scene but Khan stayed behind to pose for pictures with admirers. The next few days seemed to give good cause for his apparent self-belief. There was a solid Sunday Politics interview and an appearance alongside Baroness Doreen Lawrence, mother of the late Stephen Lawrence, the black teenager whose murder by a gang of racists in Eltham in 1993 had had profound repercussions for policing and attitudes to racism all over London. In a potent testimonial, the baroness urged voters to choose Khan and in so doing choose "hope over fear".

Meanwhile, the man Goldsmith had accused of calling for Jews to be drowned threatened him with legal action, saying the allegation was "utterly false". The Prime Minister was more supportive of the Tory candidate. He did not repeat his contested claim about Gani, which would have been risky outside the Commons, where parliamentary privilege protected him. Instead, he revived Johnson's spectre of a left-wing takeover: "Unless the voters of London act, they will feel the consequences of Corbyn's hands on the levers of power for the first time...the whole country will pay the price."

His words were carried on the front page of the Evening Standard. The following day, a report by the Media Reform Coalition and London's Goldsmiths University described the paper as a "mouthpiece of the Conservative Party" due its mayoral campaign coverage. This was assessed as "systematically biased in the way that headlines and news stories were framed, selected and prioritised". While finding that most of the Standard's news stories about the mayoral race had been neutral or balanced, the study considered that those that had shown the strongest bias were the most prominent, especially if they were negative about Khan.

The Standard's editor, Sarah Sands, had told the Guardian her paper would be "scrupulous" in giving equal prominence to the two leading candidates. She expressed surprise at the conclusions of the report. Others were not surprised at all. The Standard had been hugely supportive of Boris Johnson. Evgeny Lebedev, a collector of art and celebrities, was both his fan and his friend. It was a foregone conclusion that Goldsmith would receive the paper's formal endorsement. Yet for all the unwelcome coverage Khan had received from an array of media outlets, every indicator pointed to him still being in the lead. Nothing his enemies had thrown at him seemed to have hurt him. That left his friends.

*****

The friendly fire that threatened Khan in the final days of April began because of Naz Shah, his fellow Muslim MP who had so famously removed George Galloway from Bradford West. It was revealed that nine months before winning the seat she had suggested in social media posts that the Israel-Palestine conflict could be resolved if Israel and its people were relocated to the US. John McDonnell had taken on Shah as his parliamentary private secretary. She immediately resigned and apologised for what she had done. But any limitation to the damage the Labour Party had sustained was soon dwarfed by what happened next. Its name was Ken Livingstone.

In a BBC Radio London interview, the former mayor whose backing Khan had welcomed and touted when seeking to become Labour's candidate for 2016, came to Shah's defence. He claimed that before he "went mad" and embarked on genocide, Adolf Hitler had supported Zionism by seeking to have Germany's Jews moved to where Israel would later be founded. Whatever tendentious basis the claim had in historical fact, the crudeness with which it was expressed brought an avalanche of opprobrium down on Livingstone's head. His old friend and ally Corbyn suspended him but was accused of acting too slowly. The episode crystalised fears among Labour MPs about Corbyn's competence and some of his political stances, notably on the Middle East.

It had been bubbling in the background for some time. Now, suddenly, Labour was immersed in a full-scale anti-Semitism row. Nine days earlier, criticisms Khan had made of the process by which Livingstone had been suspended for his "concentration camp" comment to a Jewish Evening Standard reporter in 2006 had been unearthed and described as showing he had "backed" Livingstone over the remark itself.

Khan moved quickly. There was no room for even a scintilla of doubt about his view of the latest Livingstone furore. He was among the first to condemn what the former mayor had said. On Twitter he call his comments "appalling and inexcusable" adding that: "There must be no place for this in our party." A lot of his strenuous work trying to neutralise the Livingstone legacy among Jewish Londoners was under threat – and from Livingstone himself. Unlike Goldsmith's, his campaign had made few bespoke overtures to ethnic minority groups, but Jewish Londoners had been the big exception. This had brought Khan important rewards.

In January, Jewish Chronicle commentator Marcus Dysch had contrasted Khan's hunger for the job of mayor with the insouciance of Goldsmith, remarking on the Labour man's "detailed knowledge of London Jews' concerns" and how he'd distanced himself from Livingstone. "On the current evidence," wrote Dysch, "it is Mr Khan who has made the most attractive approach". Following a London Jewish Forum hustings on 5 April, which both Khan and Goldsmith had attended, Jack Mendel of Jewish News had applauded Khan for having "worked overtime" to win the backing of Jewish Londoners despite a "mounting list of problems" with the Labour Party. By contrast, Mendel judged Goldsmith to be "simply lying low".

At the end of the day of Livingstone's Hitler remark, Khan and Goldsmith went to the Copper Box indoor arena on the Queen Elizabeth Olympic Park to take part in the London Citizens Mayoral Accountability Assembly, one of the great occasions of every London mayor campaign. London Citizens is a multi-faith social action group, originating in the East End. The fervour and high emotion of the Mayoral Assembly can both exhilarate and unnerve even seasoned politicians, as formidable clerics and youthful idealists politely but sternly invite them to sign up to the Citizens' goals and work with them to see they are achieved.

It was an occasion made for Khan. The 6,000 mostly young people banked round the hall gave him a big welcome as he mounted the stage constructed at its centre and added a Muslim greeting to his general big hello. The Citizens' Assembly offer is one that candidates refuse at the cost of a polite but very public dressing down. Khan's 50% affordable policy on housing and his stridency on low pay fitted his hosts' list of requirements more precisely than those of Goldsmith, who had no option but to finesse his less compliant policies as best he could.

After young refugees had spoken of their yearning to remain in the city where they had grown up, Khan said to loud cheers that in his role as Tooting MP he had just the other night helped try to change the government's Immigration Bill so that Britain could help more unaccompanied young refugee children stranded in mainland Europe. That was the reason given for his missing an important National Housing Federation hustings held on the same evening as the Commons vote. Goldsmith hadn't been at the housing debate either, but his excuse, according to his stand-in, was that he had to meet someone in Hillingdon.

At the end, Goldsmith left quietly in the company of Nick de Bois and almost no one else.

He had the air of a lost stork trying to find its way back to Kew. Meanwhile, on the other side of the venue, the diminutive Khan disappeared into a crush of well-wishers, camera crews and selfie-seekers. He'd empathised. He'd rocked the house.

These images had an intoxicating quality. Khan had spoken the language of London's idealistic multi-ethnic polyglot and done so triumphantly at the eastern frontier of the city's growth, just a short walk from the Olympic stadium where Somalia-born Mo Farah, whom Khan had been known to cite as an inspiration, had won double Olympic gold for Great Britain four years before. There was a bellwether mood. Here was London's future. How could Khan lose?

Yet the city's diversity also embraces Havering's Essex borderland, the pebble-dash semis of John Betjeman's Metro-land and the leisured prosperity of Goldsmith's Richmond. At the Copper Box a young black couple, looking on at Khan, spoke warily of a London equivalent of the Bradley Effect, a term coined after the 1982 election to be governor of California, when black candidate Tom Bradley, the then Mayor of Los Angeles, was defeated despite opinion polls showing him ahead. Some of the white voters who'd said they would vote for him turned out to have done otherwise.

Meanwhile, Boris Johnson was making the most of Labour's discomfort over anti-Semitism. "It seems to me there's an ideological continuum between the views of Ken Livingstone about Israel, the position of Jeremy Corbyn and indeed the views of their candidate for London Mayor Sadiq Khan," he declared. Livingstone had given the Tories a new way to tie Khan to Corbyn and a wider sense of murk and menace. Johnson was not alone in exploiting it.

Eight

May

On 1 May, readers of the Mail on Sunday were treated to an article by Goldsmith. Its headline asked:

> *"On Thursday, are we really going to hand the world's greatest city to a Labour party that thinks terrorists is its friends?"*

The grammatical error was glaring. Yet the implied charge against Khan rendered it a muted shade of fawn. An accompanying photograph compounded the headline's fluorescence. It was of the London bus blown up in the 7/7 attacks.

Goldsmith's article began: "London stands on the brink of a catastrophe, the shockwaves from which would be felt across the country." A litany of impending devastation was breathlessly composed from a compendium of strained connections: an extreme case of "links" over-reach.

A Khan win, according to Goldsmith, would mean "London's £600bn economy would fall into the hands of a man who backed Ken Livingstone over his suspension in 2006 for anti-Semitic remarks to a Jewish reporter". The insinuation that Khan was in sympathy with anti-Semitism was toxic. The notion that upon election a London Mayor holds the crucible of UK free enterprise like a plaything in his palm was so fantastical that it might have been induced by LSD.

"Khan has flatly refused to rule out hiking taxes," Goldsmith went on, "which would deal a devastating blow to the engine room of the British economy". This seemed to overstate the effects of varying the mayoral council tax precept. Boris Johnson had made several reductions in it, including one shortly before the 2012 election. It saved London households in properties of average value £3.10 a year, or slightly less than a penny a day. A Labour London Assembly member had worked out that this would buy one onion a month.

Goldsmith did not set out in his article how many onions Khan would have to deprive London's £600bn economy of before capitalism ground to a halt. Perhaps that was because the allure of terror-mongering was too strong. Goldsmith succumbed to it, wantonly: "If Labour wins on Thursday we will have handed control of the Met, and with it control over national counter terrorism policy, to a party whose candidate and current leadership have, whether intentionally or not, repeatedly legitimised those with extremist views."

Again, the fabric of the case had a see-thru quality. The UK Home Secretary seemed unlikely to casually toss sole responsibility for counter-terror to any London Mayor. Goldsmith's warning also raised intriguing questions. How, precisely, did he think Khan would set about weakening London's security arrangements? Had he foreseen the agent of "aggressive socialism" putting in an early call to Sir Bernard Hogan-Howe and asking him to maybe slacken things up a bit so that fanatics could commit atrocities with greater ease? Had he imagined Hogan-Howe assuring the new mayor that he would see to it that the capital's defences were lowered right away?

The combination of the headline, the 7/7 image and Goldsmith's words sparked some sharp reactions. The most striking was on Twitter from Sayeeda Warsi, a Tory baroness who had resigned from Cameron's cabinet in 2014 over his policy towards the Middle East conflict: "This is not the @ZacGoldsmith I know. Are we @Conservatives fighting 2 destroy Zac or fighting to win this election?"

The inventive belligerence of Goldsmith's column, so at odds with his winning image as a cool, moderate Conservative, was not sustained during the final four days of the campaign. Interviewed live by Tim Donovan on the Sunday Politics with his Mail on Sunday article still fresh off the presses he was pinned down to stating unequivocally that, despite Boris Johnson's "continuum" argument, he did not believe Khan was anti-Semitic and did not believe Khan held extreme views.

Yet he stoutly continued to defend his campaign, still insisting it was valid to question Khan's past judgments. He rejected the idea that it was better to lose the election with honour than in the way he looked like losing it. He was unable to promise that he wouldn't put up public transport fares. He said he believed he was gathering momentum. He looked a little fragile and very tired.

As the betting markets showed only minimal drift away from Khan in the aftermath of the Livingstone furore, the number of viewings of a YouTube clip that had originally been posted in the first half of April suddenly surged to over 30,000. It featured Goldsmith attending the Asian Awards ceremony being interviewed about Bollywood, the sobriquet for the Hindi language film industry. "I'm a Bollywood fan," said Goldsmith into the camera: "So anything with a Bollywood theme, I will lap it up." Did this Bollywood fan have a favourite Bollywood actor or Bollywood film? "I'm not going to be able to..." Goldsmith began, and looked away, brow furrowed as if weighing a great range of equally deserving options. He turned back: "No, I'm afraid I'm not going to be able to give you one." Could he think of a single Bollywood film or actor? "I can't think of a favourite," he replied.

On the morning of 3 May, two days before the vote, he appeared on LBC. The previous evening,

Leicester City Football Club had become the English Premier League champions. At the beginning of the season their chances had been rated at 5000/1. Their triumph was sensational. Unfashionable and lacking the lavish financial resources of the league's elite, Leicester had written and starred in a classic tale of underdogs having their day. Goldsmith took it as a reference point. Asked how he rated his chances of becoming mayor, he said he was "hoping to do a Leicester City here: zoom in from behind and win on 5 May". But Leicester hadn't "zoomed in" from anywhere – they'd been at the top of the table since January.

Goldsmith took a call. A listener named Ali asked him why he had run "such a vile, disgusting Islamophobic campaign". Ali listed the literature aimed at Tamils, Sikhs and Indians and wondered why Muslims hadn't received such material too. He accused Goldsmith and the Prime Minister of maligning Suliman Gani and of using Khan's background against him. Goldsmith assured Ali that he was mistaken. All of that was just mischief made by Labour. "They want the Muslim communities of London to feel marginalised," he said: "It is completely irresponsible and it's wrong."

But in some parts of the media Goldsmith's campaign tactics now rivalled the "extremist links" of Khan as a top story. A young reporter for BBC Newsnight, Secunder Kermani, intercepted Goldsmith on a street in Wimbledon.

"Zac. Do you feel comfortable with the prominence of race in this electoral campaign?"

"I'm not doing interviews at this moment."

"Do you feel comfortable or not?"

"I'm comfortable with the campaign. Good campaign. Good positive campaign."

"Zac. Everyone's saying, 'this isn't you'. Do you regret taking on Lynton Crosby's firm to run your campaign?"

Goldsmith hung back, took a step off the kerb, buttoned his jacket, smiled painfully and said quietly: "Come on..."

Kermani said: "Sayeeda Warsi obviously thinks you're, well, effectively letting yourself down. Is she being oversensitive on race issues?"

"It's been a completely positive campaign. And it will remain so."

"What about the long term impact this might have on your reputation?"

Goldsmith looked plaintively towards the skyline.

"How do you think the Muslim constituents of London feel about your campaign?" Kermani pressed. "I've spoken to many who feel alienated and say they've been put off from going into politics."

"Come on, that's nonsense," protested Goldsmith.

"These are people we've spoken to! We've put on air on Newsnight!"

"Thanks very much," came a female voice, brightly, sprightly, slightly strained. She moved into the picture, stepping between the candidate and his interrogator: "Thanks very much. Goodnight." She ushered Goldsmith into someone's house.

Kermani's interview seemed to capture something in Goldsmith: a weariness; a longing to be somewhere else. He appeared at a rally at a state school in his constituency with Johnson and Cameron for company, both of them working hard on pretending to still be friends as EU referendum hostilities intensified. Goldsmith's mother, Lady Annabel, was there too.

Cameron told the audience that all they needed to know was that Sadiq Khan had nominated Jeremy Corbyn: "If you want to be lab rats in Labour's experiment with London then you go for the other guy." He'd first made the "lab rats" analogy back in January. He could not be faulted for consistency. Goldsmith had by then described as "inappropriate" the Mail On Sunday's choice of photograph to accompany his fiery polemic. He'd stuck by the words he'd written, though. Every one.

*****

For Khan, the last few days of the campaign were less clamorous but perhaps more nervous. The Evening Standard endorsed Goldsmith, as expected, though not as warmly as he might have hoped. The paper's editorial, after assuring readers that the paper had "done its best to be even-handed over the course of the campaign," judged Khan to have fought "the stronger and more combative campaign". And there was further praise for the Labour man: "He has dealt creditably with questions about his perceived association with extremists by emphasising his commitment to deal robustly with those who seek to harm us. Indeed, it is to his advantage that he is Muslim: a London Muslim mayor would signify that this is a unified and cohesive city."

In fact, in the end, the Standard leader seemed to suggest there wasn't much to choose between them. A tie-breaker was required. The final choice came down to beauty: "There will be many more homes built whoever is mayor, but with Mr Goldsmith it will be in the context of a coherent aesthetic." Such considerations do matter, of course, though especially so to people of aesthetic refinement called Evgeny.

The polls, though, kept calling Khan's name. A Survation survey at the end of April had been the second in a row to put him 20 points ahead. It had, though, been conducted before the Livingstone row. Khan had publicly accepted that that might hurt him. Word from some Labour activists confirmed this as a possibility. Three more polls published in early May gave Khan second round leads of 12 or 14 points, but memories of Ed Miliband's undoing were still strong.

Turnout would be crucial: a high one by Conservative voters and a low one by Labour's could spell bad news for Khan. Although the pollsters had called London right a year before, some Labour supporters could not rule out the existence of an iceberg of anti-Muslim feeling lurking undetected beneath London's multi-cultured surface that might do deadly harm. But by the eve of polling day there was little more the candidate and his team could do but make sure that the party's formidable ground force was primed to get the vote out the next day.

The morning of 5 May was sunny and still. Londoners went to the polls.

Nine

Results

The counting of votes for the London Mayor and the London Assembly does not begin until the day after the elections take place. And so on Friday 6 May at 8:00 am the first ballot boxes were unsealed at the three counting centres: Alexandra Palace, a Victorian entertainment venue near the North London suburb of Muswell Hill; the Olympia exhibition centre in West Kensington to the west of the city's centre, built during the same era; and the ExCel centre in the redeveloping docklands of East London, opened in 2000. Soon, online bar charts of verified ballot papers began to show Khan ahead on first preference votes. Updated, they showed Goldsmith ahead. Then Khan again. Then still Khan. Still Khan. Still Khan. By early afternoon, only one thing was in doubt – the size of Khan's victory. By mid-afternoon it was clear it would be huge.

The figures had settled into a telling pattern. Khan's share of first preferences hovered at around 44% and Goldsmith's at around 35%. These percentages precisely matched the respective shares of the general election vote Labour and the

Conservatives had won in London almost exactly one year before. The first glance inference was obvious: nothing Goldsmith's campaign and its press supporters had thrown at Khan had stopped Labour-leaning London from leaning the Labour candidate's way.

A possible clue to the reason lay in the turnout figures emerging from the London Assembly constituency results. The figure for Bexley and Bromley was 41%. For Greenwich and Lewisham it was 45%, for Brent and Harrow 43%, for City and East 42%. For Barnet and Camden it was 48%, despite an administrative error leading to many Barnet voters who arrived at polling stations early being turned away. For Merton and Wandsworth, which contained Khan's parliamentary seat of Tooting, it was a striking 50%. The latter was the only one of the 14 constituency seats to change hands – Labour gained it from the Conservatives, taking their total to nine. The Tories won the other five. The official turnout figure for the mayoral election was just over 46%. The absence of "Boris" and "Ken" or other big name politicians in the race had caused pundits to predict something depressingly lower than 2012, when only 38% of London electors made the effort.

The beautiful election day weather will have helped push it up, probably to Khan's advantage. And maybe the emotive nature of the debate reduced apathy levels. The completeness of

Goldsmith's failure was underlined by the fact that his campaign had dragged that debate on to its chosen ground – the religion and trustworthiness of Khan. Yet it had done him no good at all.

Among journalists at the count, a joke was doing the rounds. Credit for its coinage can almost certainly be claimed by Sunder Katwala of British Future – a think tank concerned with the integration and identity of the nation's ethnic minorities – for a remark he made to the Financial Times, published the day before the vote. Katwala had previously been general secretary of the Fabian Society. Fittingly, it was he who had suggested to Khan that he wrote Fairness, Not Favours, his Fabian pamphlet of 2008 urging the state to engage properly with British Muslims and British Muslims to engage more with mainstream civil society.

Steven Norris, the former Conservative MP who had lost the mayoral elections of 2000 and 2004 to Ken Livingstone, had made a remark similar to Katwala's. The joke evolved as it passed through many mouths. Its shortest form was this: "It's no good dog whistling in a city with no dogs." The point was made, and with almost comically good timing - on the very day the mayoral votes were counted, Lynton Crosby went to Buckingham Palace to receive a knighthood for services to politics. The truth, though, might have had a bit more to it than the joke allowed. Maybe everyone could hear the whistle and maybe some had obeyed its call. But if so, just as many had defied it.

*****

It had become a feature of mayoral election counts that the result was officially declared far later than advertised. In both 2008 and 2012 candidates and their supporters had had to wait several hours longer than expected, hanging around City Hall till deep into the night. In 2016, the tradition was maintained.

"Small discrepancies" were found in the vote totals of each mayoral candidate. Time passed. In City Hall's second floor debating chamber, a temporary stage was set up. Someone remarked that it looked like the set for a school play. At around 11:30, Jeff Jacobs, the Greater London Authority's chief officer, stepped up to the metal lectern at the front of it and announced the result of the Londonwide list part of the London Assembly election. After the numbers were read out, the eleven winners were called forward in accordance with the pecking order conferred by the mystery mathematics of d'Hondt.

Siân Berry came top. Peter Whittle was second. Caroline Pidgeon came third. The remaining eight AMs elected in this way comprised one more Green, one more from Ukip, but no more for the Lib Dems, plus three from Labour and three Conservatives, bringing their total London Assembly representations to twelve and eight respectively. The Tories elected in this way included Andrew Boff, who'd battled Goldsmith to be mayoral candidate. He'd just been on television saying the Goldsmith campaign's attempts to link Khan to alleged extremists had "blown up bridges" that he and fellow Tories had been trying to build with London's Muslim communities: "It was effectively saying that people of conservative religious views are not to be trusted and you should not share a platform with them. That's outrageous. If you are a London politician, this is just a bizarre thing to do." Boff wasn't alone in this assessment. Outgoing fellow Conservative AM Roger Evans, who had been Mayor Johnson's statutory deputy, said he was "concerned that the campaign we've run is going to leave a negative legacy which we in London are going to have to clear up long after the people who ran Zac Goldsmith's campaign have gone on their way".

The stage emptied. A few of the photographers lay on the floor and snatched some sleep. May 6 became May 7. Khan's wife and some family members took their places in prominent seats. The photographers woke up. Jacobs returned shortly after midnight, followed by nine of the twelve mayoral candidates. He read out the first preference votes. Goldsmith received 909,755. Khan received more than a million, though it took Jacobs two attempts to convey how many more as the cheers of Khan's supporters engulfed his words. At last, silence returned. Khan's first preference score was 1,148,716. The lead was unassailable.

Jacobs completed the list of twelve mayoral runners. Siân Berry finished third with 150,673 votes. This, together with the two assembly seats, meant the Greens had repeated their feat of 2012 and consolidated their presence in City Hall. Caroline Pidgeon had received 120,005 votes to put her fourth ahead of Peter Whittle on 94,373. Women's Equality Party candidate Sophie Walker came sixth with 53,055. Impressively, this pushed Respect's George Galloway down into seventh place. He received only 37,007 votes and did not appear on the podium.

Khan's share of the 2,596,961 valid first preference votes cast in total had not altered at the last. It was 44.2%. Goldsmith's too had stayed the same at 35%. Jacobs performed what was by then the formality of adding valid second preference votes to the first preference piles of the top two. Goldsmith's increased by 84,859 to 994,614. Khan's went up by almost twice as much: 161,427, bringing his final score to 1,310,143 – the largest personal mandate secured by any politician in UK history. The percentage split was in line with what the last three polls of the campaign had anticipated: Khan 56.8%, Goldsmith 43.2%, a margin of 13.6%.

Jacobs completed his numerical duties: "I therefore declare Sadiq Khan to be elected as the new Mayor of London."

It was a landslide win; a hammering. Khan's was the second biggest victory in the history of London Mayors, falling not far short of the 57.9% to 42.1% by which Livingstone had won the inaugural contest as an independent in 2000. Khan stepped forward. "Thank you, London," he said as applause gave way to his victory speech. "London is the greatest city in the world," he began, but this time it was not "at a crossroads". Instead, Khan said:

> "I am so proud of our city. I am deeply humbled by the hope and trust you have placed in me today. I grew up on a council estate just a few miles from here. Back then, I never dreamt that someone like me could be elected as Mayor of London. And I want to say thank you to every single Londoner for making the impossible possible today.
>
> I have a burning ambition for London – an ambition that will guide me every day as mayor of our great city. I want every single Londoner to get the opportunities that our city gave to me and my family – the opportunities not just to survive, but to thrive: the opportunities to build a better future for you and your family, with a decent

and affordable home and a comfortable commute you can afford; more jobs with better pay; not just being safe, but feeling safe; cleaner air and a healthier city; and the opportunities for all Londoners to fulfil their potential.

You know, I've been thinking a lot about my late dad today. He was a wonderful man and a great dad. He would have been so proud today – proud that the city he chose to call his home has now chosen one of his children to be the mayor. I want to say thank you to my amazing mum – she really is – and to my wonderful wife, my daughters and to my family. Without you, I wouldn't be here today.

And I want to say thank you to everyone who worked so hard on this election. To my campaign team - we've run a positive campaign and we've worked our socks off. I want to thank all the other campaign teams too – to every assembly candidate from every party, to the police, the returning officer and all the staff who've made the election happen. And, of course, to all the other mayoral candidates."

RESULTS

There came a short pause:

> *"This election was not without controversy. And I am so proud that London has today chosen hope over fear and unity over division. I hope..."*

He was interrupted by more Labour cheers.

> *"I hope that we will never be offered such a stark choice again. Fear does not make us safer. It only makes us weaker. And the politics of fear is simply not welcome in our city.*
>
> *I'm going to end by making a promise to London, a promise I first made during the campaign but a promise that I will keep here in City Hall. I promise to always be a mayor for all Londoners; to work hard to make life better for every Londoner, regardless of your background and to do everything in my power to ensure you get the opportunity that our incredible city gave to me. Thank you very much."*

Now Goldsmith came forward:

> *"Thank you. I want to start very simply by thanking everyone across London who's*

made this election run relatively smoothly and I want to thank my wonderful, inspiring team and the thousands of volunteers who've given up so much of their time to help my campaign over the last few months, it has been a pleasure, it's been an honour, to work with you.

But above all I want to thank the hundreds of thousands of people who trusted me today with their votes. I'm disappointed, of course, by the result, that I won't be able to deliver a manifesto that I'm really proud of: a plan to make London the greenest and cleanest city in the world, a plan to keep our city moving and growing, a plan to keep our city safe.

I want to pay tribute to all my fellow candidates and in particular I congratulate Sadiq Khan. I wish him well as he sets out to build on the successes that we've seen under Boris Johnson and to take them even further. Thank you very much."

As the candidates left the stage, something had changed since that October day when Goldsmith and Khan stood together in Parliament Square. The little guy had grown in stature. The posh boy looked small.

*****

On Saturday morning, Khan stepped on to an older and more impressive stage not far along the south bank of the Thames from City Hall. Southwark Cathedral, albeit in earlier built forms, has stood in its location right next to Borough Market and London Bridge since the 13th century. Already in attendance were Ed Miliband, numerous fellow Labour politicians, Caroline Pidgeon, Siân Berry, Transport for London's communications chief and Met commissioner Sir Bernard Hogan-Howe, who, if he had been asked by Khan to kindly make London more susceptible to terrorist attacks, was concealing his astonishment splendidly.

The Met chief would inform a reporter that he had "no concerns at all" about working with Khan. Earlier, on the radio, Michael Fallon had been unable to bring himself to say that London would be safe in the hands of the new mayor. His grudging attitude was not the first to be expressed. The mayoral candidate of a fringe far right party had turned his back on Khan when he'd made his City Hall victory speech.

The packed audience was first addressed by the cathedral's Dean, Andrew Nunn. He thanked Khan for arranging his formal signing-in to be held, not at City Hall as usual, but "in this special place". He ran through some of the cathedral's history.

Shakespeare had worshipped there. Nelson Mandela and Desmond Tutu had opened new facilities there. In earlier centuries the church had set up schools and in 1991 had dedicated a chapel to those living with or affected by HIV and AIDS.

Nunn said the cathedral sought to be "a holy place for all people, regardless of age, gender, ethnicity, sexual orientation or ability". Or, clearly, of faith. Seated at Nunn's side were representatives of all London's main religions, from Judaism, to Hinduism to the Protestant nonconformism of the Salvation Army. Nunn said: "I can't tell you how delighted I was to receive a call asking if we would be willing to host this event, as Mayor Sadiq Khan begins his term of office – our first Muslim mayor."

This prompted a standing ovation. After that, Doreen Lawrence introduced Khan. She repeated his post-midnight words about unity beating division and hope conquering fear. Khan waited in his dark blue suit and white, open-necked shirt. When he stepped forward he simply said: "My name is Sadiq Khan and I'm the Mayor of London."

This brought the house down too. Following his short speech, Khan took a pen and, guided by Jeff Jacobs, formally signed his acceptance of the duties and responsibilities of his office. News of his triumph had travelled round the world. The next day, Khan had work to do.